The Diluted Church

The Diluted Church

Calling Believers To Live Out Of Their True Heritage

Timothy L. Price

Ekklesia Press
Lincoln, Nebraska USA

The Diluted Church
Calling Believers to Live out of Their True Heritage
By: Timothy L. Price

Library of Congress Control Number: 2005923928

Publisher's Cataloging-in-Publication
(Provided by Quality Books, Inc.)

Price, Timothy L.
    The diluted church : calling believers to live out of their true heritage / Timothy L. Price.
        p. cm.
    Includes bibliographical references and index.
    ISBN 0-9765222-0-9

    1. Christianity and politics--United States.
    2. Christian conservatism--United States. 3. Church and state--United States. I. Title.

BR115.P7P755 2005   261.7'0973
                           QBI05-200037

This volume is printed on acid free paper and meets ANSI Z39.48 standards.

Scripture quotes are from The New American Standard Bible (**NASB**), © by the Lockman Foundation 1960, 1962, 1963, 1968, 1971, 1972, 1973, 1975, 1977. Other versions include either New King James Version (**NKJV**) or King James Version (**KJV**)

Jacket Design by: **Nate Perry**
Photographs on front and back cover by: **Greg Hendrickson**

Printed in the United States of America

Ekklesia Press is a ministry to help authors get published and to publish works that are not deemed "profitable" by the mainstream publishing industry. Our goal is to put works into print that will impact and motivate followers of Christ to fulfill the Great Commission in an ever increasing way.

Ekklesia Press is an extension of www.kingdomcitizenship.org

Ekklesia Press
P.O. Box 5935
Lincoln, NE, 68505 USA

Contents

I would like to thank many people in regards to finishing this book. It's doubtful that I could have started or even finished without each one of you.

To: Pastor Elmer Murdoch, Dr. David Rambo, Nate Krupp, Betty Daffin, Winkie Pratney, Ray Mayhew, Billy Dixon, Charlie Pugh, Jeff & Randy Brown, Kyle & Gail Knapp, my cousin Eleanor Wright, Chris Smith, Andrew Baker, Pastor Bob Kneff, Burton Holland, for making suggestions, and helping me to shape this work and make it practical.

To: Rollie Rexilius and Joe Burkey for encouraging me for years to write this book.

To: Gary Peterson, Betty Whitworth, Joyce Bjork and Wilma Bell for help in editing/proofing.

To: My wife Pam, and our kids, for letting me do this arduous process called writing.

To: Patrick Kasuule of Uganda for getting me started in thinking outside the box and bringing an outside mind into the discussion which reveals how political the church is in this country really is.

There are countless others who I could thank. But suffice it to say in both negative and positive ways many have helped to bring this book to fruition.

To God be the glory!

– Foreword –

The Diluted Church is a very important book for our generation. It addresses a number of fundamental errors in thinking and practice that have become embedded in the fabric of Christianity in America. If the Church had not strayed so far from its Gospel moorings, a book like this would be unnecessary. However, so many Fundamentalist, Evangelical and Charismatic leaders have taken their cues from sources other than Scripture that we have before us a legion of religious agendas saturated with confusion and peppered with falsehood.

In all the current clamor to "reclaim our culture" and "bring America back to God," have we not forgotten a very important perspective? Peter noted, "For it is time for judgment to begin with the household of God; and if it begins with us, what will be the outcome for those who do not obey the gospel of God?" (1 Pet. 4:17; cf. 1 Cor.5:9-13). How dare we expend precious energies and resources toward putting band-aids on a corrupt culture, when the visible Church is admittedly in such disarray? It is easy for preachers to point their fingers towards those on the streets and become red in the face as they parade the litany of evils present in society. It is much more difficult for church leaders to deal with the serious problems going on among those who sit in comfortable pews and stand behind pulpits.

In this regard, D.M. Lloyd-Jones astutely observed:

> I have no hesitation again in asserting that the failure of the Church to have a greater impact upon the lives of men and women in the world today is due entirely to the fact that her own life is not in order. To me there is nothing more tragic or short-sighted or lacking in insight than the assumption, made by so many, that the Church herself is all right and all she has to do is to evangelize the world outside. Every revival proves clearly that people who are outside the Church always become attracted when the Church herself begins to function truly as the Christian Church . . . So we must start with ourselves . . . (*Studies in the Sermon on the Mount*, Vol.1, p.54).

How can we devote valuable time and talent to "re-establishing the Judeo-Christian heritage in our culture" when the Church itself is in such a mess? *The Diluted Church* helps us to face this question squarely in light of God's Word.

Many have come to acknowledge that the Church has lost its edge because of its attachment to and accommodation with American affluence. "At ease in Zion" seems to be a very appropriate phrase to summarize Christianity in the United States. The historian Thomas C. Reeves isolates some of the key characteristics that mark church-going folks:

> But most of us, it seems clear, expend the great bulk of our time and energies fulfilling the American dream. We are consumed by our jobs . . . and are locked into an endless pursuit of the power, cash, status, and pleasure that promise "personal fulfillment" and happiness. Probably few clergy address this issue (there is

the budget to meet and the new parish hall to be built), and, as Robert Wuthnow puts it, "we therefore go about our lives pretty much the same as those who have no faith at all" . . . Christianity in modern America is, in large part, innocuous. It tends to be easy, upbeat, convenient, and compatible. It does not require self-sacrifice, discipline, humility, an otherworldly outlook, a zeal for souls, a fear as well as love of God. There is little guilt and no punishment, and the payoff in heaven is virtually certain. The faith has been overwhelmed by the culture, producing what may be called cultural Christianity . . . [that is] when the faith is dominated by a culture to the point that it loses much or most of its authenticity . . . What we now have might be best labeled Consumer Christianity . . . Millions of Americans today feel free to buy as much of the full Christian faith as seems desirable. The cost is low and customer satisfaction seems guaranteed . . . America is not – not yet, anyway – a thoroughly secular society. But its Christianity, in large part, has been watered down and is at ease with basic secular premises about personal conduct and the meaning of life. Such a religion has an uncertain future for it has absorbed ideas and attitudes that may well lead to its demise. Authentic Christianity and the world are by definition at odds, (*The Empty Church: Does Organized Religion Matter Anymore?*, The Free Press, 1996, pp. 66,67).

This is not a pretty picture. Where can we find a Christ-exalting alternative to this anemic situation? Again, *The Diluted Church* provides a solid Biblical framework that calls us to pursue what is necessary for authentic Gospel faith to flourish.

The pressure is mounting for the Church to trust in chariots and horses such as trivial gimmicks, politics, and militarism in order to accomplish certain alleged spiritual ends. To just trust the Holy Spirit to bless and prosper the Word of God is too iffy and does not usually produce quick, visible results. Eric Hoffer has pointed out the propensity of various causes to employ power-tactics.

> There is hardly an example of a mass movement achieving vast proportions and a durable organization solely by persuasion . . . It was the temporal sword that made Christianity a world religion. Conquest and conversion went hand in hand . . . Where Christianity failed to gain or retain the backing of state power, it achieved neither a wide nor a permanent hold . . . It also seems that, where a mass movement can either persuade or coerce, it usually chooses the latter. Persuasion is clumsy and its results uncertain (*The True Believer*, Mentor, 1964, pp. 100, 101).

When the Church becomes more driven by cultural forces than by the Lord's Word, the Gospel is always watered down. The Church rests contentedly within the general morality of a civil religion, minus Jesus. Instead of being counter-cultural, the Church is acculturated. The God of the Bible is conveniently merged with all the other gods of America, so that no one is offended. Can we be satisfied with such a culturally-defined deity?

In a recent column, commentator Nicholas Van Hoffman wrote about the Mush God who caters to all tastes. He stated that President Carter, who normally identifies with the more jealous God of evangelical Christianity, reaffirmed his faith in the great non-denominational Mush God at the recent White House

Prayer Breakfast. Hoffman describes the Mush God as follows:

"The Mush God has been known to appear to millionaires on golf courses, to politicians at ribbon-cutting services and to clergymen speaking the invocation on national television at either the Democratic or Republican conventions. The Mush God's presence is felt during Brotherhood Week and when Rotarians come together. He is the vapid deity President Carter was referring to when suggesting peace might come to the Middle East because the Egyptian president and Israeli prime minister both worship the great mushy one. The Mush God has no theology to speak of, being a Cream of Wheat divinity. The Mush God has no particular credo, no tenets of faith, nothing that would make it difficult for believer and non-believer alike to lower one's head when the temporary chairman tells us that Reverend, Rabbi, Father, Mufti or So-and-So will lead us in an innocuous prayer, for this god of public occasions is not a jealous god. You can even invoke him to start a hookers' convention and he/she or it won't be offended. God of the Rotary, God of the Optimists Club, Protector of the Buddy System, the Mush God is the Lord of secular ritual, of the necessary but hypocritical forms and formalities that hush the divisive and derisive. The Mush God is a serviceable god whose laws are chiseled on tablets but written on sand, amenable to amendment, qualification and erasure. This is a god that will compromise with you, make allowances and declare all wars holy, all peace sacrosanct (from *Sources & Resources*, 1978).

The Diluted Church calls us to forsake the culturally-rooted Mush God and to love and follow the Living God and Father of our Lord Jesus Christ. I pray that this book will be used by the Lord to awaken many to seek first the Kingdom of God, and to flee from the numerous agendas backed by many church leaders that ultimately rely upon the arm of the flesh.

Jon Zens, Editor, *Searching Together*
www.searchingtogether.org

Introduction

There is much talk by church people these days about politics. Then again, there have been few moments in history when politics wasn't an important topic of conversation. To think that there is an under emphasis on politics in today's church is a vast understatement. Few topics achieve a higher priority or regularity in our talk.

Daily, popular talk radio shows raise one issue after another which ultimately have implications in politics or seek a solution in the political arena. You can hardly turn on a radio to religious stations without being barraged with some sort of active political issue. Words are tossed about on these shows that create feelings of fear, ownership in the state, responsibility and a host of other motivations. In political discussions in religious circles there is more reference given to the Founding Fathers of America than the Apostles or Early Church Fathers. It seems as if Thomas Jefferson and Benjamin Franklin have greater meaning to the followers of Christ than scripture does.

Without question these inadvertent correlations by religious political people are intended in the best way possible. I do not think anyone means to imply that George Washington and the others are more important to us than the Apostles or Christ. However, if we're not careful maybe there are subtleties here taking on more importance than we mean. Just how important should the founding of America be to followers of Christ residing in this country? This is not clear. The incessant adoring talk on this subject, in our churches and channels of teaching, indicates that few are grappling with any question about the prevalence of this extolment, or the implication of what this means.

Another question we should consider: do we really have Biblical warrant for attempting to "change culture" through politics as many teach these days? Can we overemphasize a few scriptures in this pursuit while denying many more at the same time? We can certainly find historical support for what is being preached today about political activism. Are we using these examples as the "proof texts" for our actions instead of the Word of God? Can God bless someone's work at one point in history without that blessing being viewed as an authoritative basis for using the same approach today? God uses many people's actions, but that does not mean that He sanctions what they do.

On another front, what fails in our work as followers of Christ if we should become high-centered on the political arena as our main area of conquest? Could there be such a thing as high-centered? Are there extremes concerning this topic of church/state relations? If so what are they and who is promoting them? If there are extremes then what about balance? Who is asking these kinds of questions in order to consider the whole topic comprehensively?

These are just a few of the questions I have struggled with over the years in trying to come to terms with what I read in the Bible and what I hear and see being done concerning politics by people who claim to be following Christ.

Background:

In the Spring of 1988, prior to the Primary election, I was sitting around a dorm with others at

Bible School. We were talking about the upcoming election. Each person took turns theorizing about whom they would vote for and why. One fellow said he was going to vote for Pat Robertson because Robertson was a Christian. Another said he would vote for Lamar Alexander for some other reason. Still a third said, "Bush is my man" because he had more experience and he had a good foreign policy. The pontification went on and on.

A brother from Uganda spoke up after some time. He said, "You guys are crazy! You speak about who to vote for and why, but what if God told you to vote for a Pharaoh [meaning a totally ungodly person] would you do it?" This astounded everybody! Most agreed that God would never do this kind of thing. No one accepted the possibility that God could say don't vote or worse yet –from a human point of view– vote for a "Pharaoh." This fellow shared scripture that exposed our perspectives to be different than God's. We had difficulty considering the scripture this fellow shared with us because we had already settled on our own point of view.

This situation irked me! I began to ask myself questions. I deliberated about the answers, and the reasons for the answers we normally give, concerning our political involvements. I considered the ways in which we had chosen to deal with the subject of political action in the church. The more I questioned and read the Bible for support of one view or the other, the more frustrated I became.

Historically speaking we have two main ideas to pick from in discussions of politics and the church. One extreme wants nothing to do with worldly culture and society, including politics, it's isolationistic. The other extreme is total engagement, activism and the belief in a "political savior" either through a person or corporate dominance. This second view is currently infused in the conservative religious-right. Of course there are varying degrees of these two extremes. It seems as though we are forced to choose between these two polar opposites. What about balance? What does the Bible say? Could there be more to this topic of church/state relations from a Biblical point of view than we are accustomed to understanding?

The Bible indeed has many things to say that would support one group's view. Yet, it also has things to say that support the opposite view. This forces both groups to avoid certain texts because they do not fit their separate conclusions or texts end up being twisted so that they do fit a desired view. All these scenarios bothered me. It has been since this realization that I began to understand that God in His infinite wisdom has given us two approaches to almost any subject. There are times to evoke either side and certainly a need to keep both in mind.

For many, maintaining balance between the two options is tough in a practical sense. Many feel that only one side or the other is "the truth." Either may be "the truth" we need to apply at the time. The other position is not dispensable simply because it is not needed at the time. As a practical example: when a person is legalistic in his views we can temper this extreme with grace. When a person is freewheeling and without constraint we can temper this extreme with law and discipline. Neither grace nor law is an end; both are parts of the whole truth. With respect to politics, neither total engagement nor total isolation from politics, society or culture are absolute truths that we should practice. In our own strength we can only try to counteract the extremes we see around us with our own extremes. Instead we should walk in the quiet way God leads us, regardless of the provocation to act on behalf of the moral emergency of the moment be it news, preaching or group dynamics (denominational or political).

While I do not object to the values Christian conservatives try to uphold in their efforts, I do object to how it is being done. While I do not object to holding up truth and light in this society, once again I object to how it is being done through politics, attended by the attitudes and motives connected with most political activists I have met.

If we listen to the politically active we are made to think we have a "God mandated" stewardship in state-sponsored freedom. This is not necessarily true. Even if it is true it may not be absolute. When we take a position on a subject we cannot use just the parts of the Bible that support the way we want to think. Yet, when we take as much as we can find in the Bible on a topic we are often hard pressed to come to a single conclusion. This has been the bane of church history. The point is that God needs to direct what we do. While He uses leaders in the church we know from the past that leaders can take on a mind of their own, even in well-meaning. How are we to know what our options are unless we are continually deepened by the counsel of God? Are we even listening to Him? Are we to follow mere man or are we cooperating with men as God is guiding us?

The bulk of this book is aimed at showing what the current trends in religious conservative political activity produces. Secondly, we'll look at lots of what the Bible has to say. This will show us how we can live and work in this world without becoming extremist or narrow minded. We must come to a greater under-standing of what God's Word has to say on the subject of church/state relations. When we open our ears and listen to what God is telling us about the applications of His Word to the times in which we live, we will be effective and the Kingdom's work will progress through us instead of in spite of us.

Going further, we have been commanded to evangelize the entire world and make disciples of all nations. This command has *no exceptions*. It is mandatory for all followers of Christ to play an active part. We can do all that conservatives want to do, such as stand for morality, raise awareness of what sin will bring, while we do what we've been commanded. If, however, we go at politics and culture for any other reason than God directing us to do so, we will not only fail to do what we have been commanded by God, but we will also fail in our agenda of political conquest.

We must come away from the imbalanced fringes and walk the fine line of what God wants us to do in the times we live. To rail and browbeat with only part of what the Bible tells us is to exclude God from directing the balance that we are to live. It is also the way of stepping down from truth into mere religion. Excluding God through systematic narrow thinking is also the way to give the enemy victory because we are not walking according to God's will, but our own.

Timothy L. Price

Special Note:

I have avoided naming of living people or ministries that may be promoting views questioned by the thesis of this book, other than in citing facts or statistics. The reasons for this are manifold. A person or a ministry may change their ideals over time. It is common in religious circles to literarily assassinate people in print but I do not wish to do so. Additionally, we do not learn to think about what others say if we are first inoculated against them. I would much rather that you come to understand which people and organizations are promoting ideas that are not what God wants by your own mental processes.

Section 1

Analysis

IN TIMES OF CHANGE,
LEARNERS INHERIT THE EARTH,
WHILE THE LEARNED FIND
THEMSELVES BEAUTIFULLY
EQUIPPED TO DEAL WITH A
WORLD THAT NO LONGER
EXISTS.

– Eric Hoffer –

1

Subjective Thinking
In The Camp

Who will you vote for in the next election? Was JFK really shot by just one lone assassin? Which college football team is the greatest of all time? These are just a few of the subjects on which we could have substantial opinions. Each of us has perspectives on any variety of subjects such as these. Yet, few of us have an authoritative grasp of the various subjects on which we hold formidable opinions. Most of us lack the information necessary to secure a commanding grip on all of these subjects. In order to gain a better understanding in any area we need to absorb information from others who have more experience or perspective than we do. If we do not open our minds to consider what others have to say, we run the risk of operating under false assumptions.

As an illustration of the human tendency to operate under false assumptions of ability or understanding, consider a father on Christmas morning. He proudly sets about assembling his son's new modular desk, having first tossed the directions aside. Perhaps this father has past experience in such endeavors. Maybe he possesses a good mechanical aptitude. In any case, he aggressively jumps into the assembly process only to find that his ability and experiences are falling short. He then realizes that he does not understand how this particular product is supposed to end up looking like the picture on the box.

Wouldn't you agree that this fellow is a picture of each one of us? At one point or another we have all reached beyond what our abilities or understanding allow us. It is my conviction that such is the case with modern Christians regarding the current relationship between politics and believers, i.e. the Church.

Why do we think and process information the way we do?

Most of us think the way we do because of dynamics in our formative years. Experts tell us that our frame of reference is shaped for us during our first six to eight years. By the time we can intellectually take these perspectives apart for ourselves, we are so imprinted by our original worldview that it is difficult to see outside it in order to objectively compare this view to other ideas. This can be bad because we will commonly dismiss ideas that appear to be *new* in favor of our long-held, handed-down ideas. This kind of choice is made simply on the basis of familiarity and nothing else. Even if these newly presented ideas were correct we will most commonly stave them off because they are perceived as being *totally new*, rather than just new to us.

Experience, the things that we have done, and exposure, things that we inherit by way of passive absorption, tend to be the main elements that shape our frame of reference. Experience and exposure certainly have value. Yet, the absolute trueness of any frame of reference is another question entirely. The trueness of any point of view, built solely on our personal background of education or religious perspective, can only be verified when these outlooks fit into the larger frame of reference squarely from a biblically accurate understanding. When our beliefs are based on just what our experiences and exposure afford us, we cannot say that we truly have a balanced understanding. If our background is the determining factor in the way we think, over and against what is or what can be proven to be true, we are then in the realm of what is called subjective or relative thinking.

You might have already realized that subjectivism and relativism are hallmarks of this generation. On any given day you can hear the slogans of these two *"isms"* in comments like, *that's your truth or that's your reality.* Relativism clouds people's view of what is absolute. Relativism by definition is a philosophical theory that elevates one's own position in reference to a subject rather than that subject's relationship to an absolute universe. Since the theory of relativism has its basis in a person's position in reference to the subject matter, truth is then thought to be a matter of one's own opinion rather than a matter of being true regardless of anybody's position. In short, relativism passes itself off as being positional truth,* rather than truth that is absolute.

For the followers of Jesus Christ, can adjectives be used to describe Truth?

In a day and age when relativism is the kingpin of philosophical approaches to living, even to a great degree in the church, we need to get back to absolute thinking where God provides the key to a proper perspective. It is imperative that we scrutinize whether

Footnote: Positional truth is a view based from one's perspective on the realities he sees. This is counter to truth being factual no matter a person's vantage point or interpretive means. As an example: some thinkers used to believe, even dogmatically, the earth was the center of our solar system because from their perspective it seemed so. We have learned from a larger perspective that this old view was incorrect.

some of our privately held ideas square up to the overall picture of God's plan. This scrutiny must include cherished rationale that has been handed down to us by parents or education.

To illustrate further how people can be subjective in their thinking, let us imagine a fellow who wants to erect a building in an urban setting. There are numerous details to consider in such a venture; e.g. sewer lines, roads, electrical and other utilities along with environmental impact. The land considered for a building has to be surveyed or "measured" as to its size and its make-up, i.e., what is on the land and the locations of those items. The lay of the land itself is also very important. This measuring is always done in reference to a known point of origin called a *benchmark*.

The benchmark, upon which a survey is based from is a point where certain established absolutes have been checked and checked again. The surveyor and subsequently the builders, civil inspectors or anyone else can refer back to this point at any time during the construction project. They know that this benchmark is sure. With this in mind, what would you think of our prospective builder if he disregarded such logical processes, by proceeding out to a field, shoving a stick in the ground indiscriminately, declaring that he will build his building using this point as a frame of reference. This seems egotistical, subjective and foolish doesn't it? The local city building inspector will have a field day reeling this guy into compliance with state and city codes.

With such an egocentric approach towards any subject, one can be deluded into thinking his or her personal viewpoint is absolutely, positively correct in every sense of the meaning, because their thinking is not tied to any *benchmark*. If one's perspective is limited to a independent mindset, such as with our fictitious builder, it would be wrong to say that their view was absolutely correct or balanced. We always need to prove ideas and approaches. Things must be confirmed objectively. When a philosophical mind-set is based on presupposed positions that are *validated* by a support base located in the middle of nowhere historically, logically or even biblically, it would have to be branded as subjective thinking.

A real life example of subjective thinking is the local evolutionist. They are prime showpieces of the cyclical and relativistic thinking people are willing to subscribe to because they want to, not because they have objectively proved their thinking with all of the information available. Early on evolutionists developed an elaborate dating system based on archeological discoveries and the supposition that evolution is plausible. Initially their approach based the dating of artifacts and remains on geologically associated relationships. They compared findings in one strata to findings in other strata. Then they used one layer to base the age of everything else that was found.

Being preconditioned by their theories, evolutionists suppose the universe to be very old. They then automatically presume any "find" to be very old before they would think of it as possibly being more recent. Given these presuppositions they then set about to find a means to support their views, ergo Carbon-14. The interpretive information would seem to *support* their view of reality...but does it? Long since, Carbon-14 was proven to be critically flawed and often grossly inaccurate.[1] And even though for years Carbon-14 had been totally debunked as being *junk science* on a technical and intellectual level, it is still the basis for popular opinion at street level in discussions of evolution.

This brief explanation of the evolutionists' approach to interpreting information shows that their preconceived ideas have more to do with the outcomes of their analysis than objective research. The problems with this kind of thinking are enormous! But we can see that evolutionists are expressly given to such reaches in analysis because of their preconceived ideas.

Evangelicals, Fundamentalists and Charismatics alike believe that we are above this type of thinking and living. We have all sorts of philosophical ideas that are supposed to be integral, not full of split ends. Yet, we're involved with various activities that suggest we either do not really believe some of what we teach or we do not realize that we are walking outside of our teaching. While a good bit of what is taught in our circles is good and accurate, we are not immune to the weakness of subjective thinking. We ridicule the local evolutionist while at the same time we are wallowing in a similar quagmire in our subjective methods of interpreting what we see.

Evangelicals, Fundamentalists and Charismatics have supposed for more than 40-years that the founding of America [an alleged Christian Republic] is the motivation for our various political involvements. Many leaders and lay people pursue and perform, without a thought or careful study of the Bible, an assumed duty to the state thinking they are still a part of it. They pursue this duty to the state without a clear understanding of history, or the way the Pre-Nicene church lived, or even the theological overlays that have been handed down to us directly through the Reformation of Luther, Calvin and Zwingli.

Politics is a very sophisticated activity with potential advantages for the church. At the same time there are many more pitfalls. Politics is an arena that conservatives have seized upon to effect change in society as they see fit. But it is also an arena in which, it seems, that all the costs have not been counted. In some cases counting the cost is scoffed at because the supposed advantage in politics clouds the issue.

Religious conservatives deeply desire to establish a nation that follows God's order, but they have misunderstood their true purpose and role as disciples who are to follow Christ. They have stopped short of this main objective for a purpose more of their own liking.

The outgrowth of thought that has led to the "political action" of the grass roots in the body of Christ has many directions and goals. It is like a ten-headed monster lashing out in various directions all at once. There are all sorts of views being voiced, proclaiming what to do and why to be *active* in the political arena. There are "Christians"* in all political persuasions, be it liberal, conservative, moderate or independent. Many of them are decent, conscientious people. Conservative Christians see that this country is going down the tubes. Naturally they are offering up resistance to make sure this doesn't happen.

Politically minded believers are sincere in their belief that they can turn the tide in the self-titled "culture-war" through the political arena. Their determination is admirable and well noted. Yet *well-meaning* is not a way of equating positive value to any involvement from the perspective of following Christ. Neither is good intention a determining factor for why or what we should do as followers of Christ. If well-meaning were really the standard of well-spent time and energy, we should laud the Jehovah's Witnesses and Mormons for their determination and dedication.

Broaching the motivating factors of the Religious-Right is an interesting study. When asked, the local religious conservative will give you lots of reasons as to why he or she is invested in this direction of top-down culture change. There are the perennial issues such as

*Footnote: By saying "Christian" I mean anybody who consider themselves to be Christian without any definable evidence. It is said that 86% of Americans say they are Christian. They either don't know what Christian is or we have allowed the term to become so meaningless anyone could be considered to be a Christian. Just because someone says they're a Christian does not mean anything. Where is the "fruit in keeping with repentance"?

restoring the sanctity of human life, protecting marriage to be only between opposite genders, controlling the spread of gambling, and the list goes on. All these details and more religious conservatives expect to change, reverse or protect exclusively through using the political system. As one fellow observed the phenomenon of various motives in the conservative camp, he wrote: "For if they [Christians] engage in politics...it is not out of mere interest, but out of a terrifying *arsenal of motivations* which compel them to experience a tragic agony in connection with every political event."[2] The rank and file of this movement is armed with every chart, graph, e-mail alert and book known to man. They seem to have every documented reason in the world for doing what they do, *but does this all stand up in light of God's Word?* Many suppose that it does but we must confirm this objectively.

Two specific motives that I have observed are those that history provides: belonging to and ownership of our part in America. We will deal with these points to a greater degree later in our study. Suffice it to say, history indeed tends to be a major factor in the motivation of conservatives. History is not the only culprit that predisposes believers to turn from the old and narrow path onto the wide and paved thoroughfare of political activism as the chief means of acting out their beliefs. Theology is a major contributor as well. On top of an inadequate understanding of history most of these politically active believers are not thoroughly trained in theology either. The political activists fall into practices based on theological stands, the origins of which they have no idea, all while continuing their activities gleefully with no problem.

Many of these activists, it would seem, do not think about the potential negative ramifications of what they advocate. It may seem alarmist to bring up the negative ramifications, because the historical and theological errors are not mammoth. Yet let's be reminded that it only takes but one degree of diversion to be off target by tens of thousands of miles on a trip from Earth to Mars.

If you still think these small errors are no big problem, let's put a tiny lump of pure strychnine in your coffee. Would you still indulge yourself with that cup?

The Apostle Paul put it like this: "A little leaven leavens the whole lump of dough", (*cf.* Gal. 5:9). In verse 7 preceding this text Paul asks, "You were running well; who hindered you from obeying the truth?" The leaven in the text refers to the teaching and philosophies of the Judaizers and Pharisees. Their teachings were very much "of this world." Paul's question is then very contemporary to our discussion as well.

Who has hindered the church in America from obeying the truth?

Does a recent view of history, the venerated view of America's christianized* founding, provide a motivation for the church to assault the political realm with an esoteric agenda?

Does a selected group of scriptures continually rehashed form a basis from which we should march on Washington and try to dominate the political theatre of this country?

Are Evangelicals, Fundamentalists and Charismatics any different from the evolutionist when it comes

*Footnote: Many think that America's founding was "Christian" in the best sense of the meaning. However, if being a Christian is having a personal relationship with God, it becomes impossible collectively speaking, for a nation to have that kind of relationship with God. Therefore, America at best could only be influenced by Christian thought, it can not be an institutional example set up by God such as Israel. This then debunks the concept of America attaining covenant nation status as some teachers have tried to espouse, in trying to buttress the need to go out and re-take what is ours, according to their estimation.

to using very limited perspectives and presupposed ideas to fuel our engine?

Could there be more truth from a wider frame of reference about this subject than most believers in America have thought about before?

Most people would vehemently oppose this possibility. Not because it could possibly be true, but because they perceive that if it were true it could negate their platform, cause, and possibly even their life's effort. Many have wrapped their total identity into their political endeavors. This is why religious conservative Christians wrangle so vigorously against any brethren who disagree with them concerning the need for *en masse* political activity by the church. This ire is felt even when a disagreement in approach is not antagonistic but rather an earnest pursuit of truth. I can understand people being wrapped up in the wrong things. I can even empathize with those who feel as though they may be marginalized by this discussion.

We cannot turn our backs on other possibilities in approach to politics, including abandonment for a greater purpose. We must give ear to what God is saying. The full counsel of God has not been heard on this subject, including what is in this book. This work is just another piece of the puzzle. We must consider the cost to the cause of Christ if we are incorrect in our current approaches. If we are wrong, Christ is paying secondary cost to that which He already paid on the cross for such selfishness in subjective thinking and living on our part.

2

The State Of Things In The Church In America

One of the many reasons I wrote this book is that the supposed purpose for the church as defined by Christ does not seem to be true in a practical sense for what many call "the church." I want to draw attention to this in detail and maybe show some reasons for this shortfall. If we cannot see that something is wrong with the church in America, then we need to prepare ourselves to have our doubts erased.

Several years ago a rather stinging comment was made about Evangelicals by George Verwer, the founder of one of the largest missionary groups in the world, Operation Mobilization. Verwer said, *"Evangelicals are champions for those who know everything and who do NOTHING."*[1] As we will look at the current conditions of the church in America we will see that indeed something is amiss. We will also see why Mr. Verwer can legitimately make his comment concerning the church in the West, particularly in America.

It is always good to step back and look at the condition of our endeavors (*cf.* Prov. 27:23). In the same way we should check the condition of our car to make sure it is in good shape before we go on a long trip. Our life could depend on whether our vehicle's mechanical state is like it's supposed to be. We should commonly check the tire pressure and fluid levels to see that there is enough of each so that disaster will not strike at an unexpected moment, when we are most unable to fix it. If the car's mechanical condition is left to itself, disaster will certainly take place. It is not a matter of if, it's only a matter of when.

Have you ever thought that we as believers should be checking out the condition of our involvements and approaches (our spiritual vehicle) from time to time the same as we would with a real car?

When was the last time each of us stepped back from our local part of the church mosaic in order to check the general condition of both our local fellowship and the body of Christ-at-large regarding activities, focuses, teachings and accomplishment of biblical directives? What are we getting done and is it what God intended? Where are the telltale marks in the church equivalent to an automobile's dipstick and pressure gauges? How could we tell if the church were building with wood, hay, or stubble if we do not stand back and take a real look? Fortunately, we as followers of Christ do not have to lean on those who have agendas or who have ulterior motives to find out what really is true. We have the Word of God, which is the only source of truly objective information that has not been tainted and twisted by the progressions of man.

Where Is The Dipstick?

The word "dipstick" has always been a funny term to me because it conjures thoughts of the 1980's TV sitcom: *The Dukes of Hazzard*. The show featured a crooked Mayor, some hillbilly rednecks and a couple of cops who, for the lack of a better description, were dumber than fence posts. The mayor always referred to these deputies as "dipsticks" because they were buffoons. In the current study we are not looking for ridiculously stupid people nor even an actual dipstick in a car, but rather an equivalent indicator that will help us check the status of the organized church.

We will find in statistics some indicators of what is happening in the church. While statistics can be subjective, they become very objective when they are corroborated with what the Bible tells us. When we begin to compare statistics concerning the church to the Bible's standard it will show any deficiency. While statistics fall short of reporting on each and every person, they show us trends which help compose a picture of what is prospectively true on a broad basis for any group being analyzed.

In the early 1980's, an unlikely *prophet* by the name of Keith Green came to be well-known through his music. He spoke out against the lethargy and disconnectedness that personified the church at that time. Keith used not only music but printed matter to motivate and direct an entire generation of new believers. Keith died in a plane crash in 1982 but with the advent of recordings, he still speaks today with as much applicability as he did back then.

Keith's last published work, entitled, *Why you should go to the Mission Field,* is still available. It is poetically speaking not only his last work but also was his magnum opus. He cited many statistical facts that were rather embarrassing for organized Christianity at that time. It showed the church's ineffectiveness, laziness (*Keith's words*), and how out of touch Christians were. If Keith's analysis was unbelievable back then, what is even more unbelievable is that after 20-years, the statistics are not any better.

Keith wrote, "only 9% of the world speaks English [*as their mother tongue*] and yet 94% of all ordained ministers in the whole world minister to the 9% who speak English." Continuing he wrote, "96% of all Christian finances are spent in the United States which represents only 6% of the world's population. While only 4% of all Christian money is spent on missionary efforts to reach the other 94% of the world's population."[2] George Barna, one of the leading statisticians of Christianity in America, records a modern corroborative statistic to what Keith Green wrote. Barna states that for every dollar of money spent to minister to the poor, the typical *American* church spends more than five dollars on buildings and maintenance.[3] Notice this last statistic does not include salaries, benefits or any other normal expense. What Barna is saying is that missions expenditures are only 20% of church maintenance figures, which would be comparatively less than the whole budgetable amount of the average church. That figure might be too embarrassing to print.

Going back to Keith Green, he states, "There are over 1-million full-time, [*that is paid or supported*] Christian workers in the United States; while one half the world population....2.2-Billion people, have only 2417 full-time Christian workers. [*clarification mine*] If you crunched the numbers this works out to 1 full-time Christian worker to every 450,000 people!"[4] The vast majority of missionaries on the field, then and even now, are working in places where the Gospel has been preached, in some cases for a century or more! On a more current note another research group cited that only 2-3% of all missionaries in the world work in "unreached people groups" or "hard to work with people groups", such as the Moslems, within the 10-40 window.[5]*

These facts do not stand alone; they can be corroborated with other notable sources that have also come to similar conclusions. The Global Evangelization

---

*Footnote:** This 10-40 window is a location in latitude and longitude that most missionary societies agree encompasses the vast majority of unreached/hard-to-reach people in the world.

Movement, or GEM, published similar findings to those of Keith Green, as well as the US Center for World Missions. In 1996, one study done on missionary deployment found that the United States accounted for only 26-1/2% of the world's missionaries.[6]

Considering that America is one of the richest countries in the world, don't you think the church in this country is operating disproportionately to its capability concerning missions work?

In comparison, European Union of countries as a whole sent out double the missionaries than that of the United States during the same time period. Keep in mind, people in most European countries have less money to work with than the church in America. They live in socialistic political systems that confiscate 50-60% of their earnings in taxation. In addition, they tend to be more liberal in their religious beliefs, meaning that they have even less of an evangelical motive to do missions work than the church in this country should have. It does not seem possible that this could be true, but it is.

We evangelicals say we believe the command to go, so why aren't we the ones going in droves?

When pressed about foreign missions many will say that there is much in this country to do. Agreed. However, if there is nowhere one can go in this country and not hear a message or something that gives witness to God, and there are places in the world that have never had witness, don't you think we have more responsibility to these *darker* places?

World missions is the only job that Christ gave the church, (*cf.* Matt. 28:19-20). It is at this very point that we begin to see the church in America has come into some significant problems. In 1998 George Barna published a book called: *The Second Coming of the*

Church. Barna's book provides many comparative statistics similar to those which we've already looked at, which is very interesting given our discussion of the church being off track. The information contained in this chart is nothing less than horrifying!

Chart-A

Behavior	Born-Again Christian	Non-Christian
Watched MTV, the music television channel in the last week	19%	24%
Registered to vote	83%	79%
Have been divorced (among those who have been married)	**27%**	23%
Discussed politics in the past week	41%	47%
Subscribe to Cable Television	70%	70%
Bought a lottery ticket, in the past week	**23%**	27%
Took drugs or medication prescribed for depression, in the past year	7%	8%
Watched a PG-13 or R-rated movie in the past 3 months	76%	87%
Watched an X-rated movie in the past 3 months	**9%**	16%

Chart-A downsized from original source[7]

Some of these statistical findings are outrageous! In particular, divorce being higher in the church than in the world? In addition, gambling and pornography percentages, representing what is commonly considered to be the church, are very close to that which should only be an identification of the secular population? What has happened to the church!

The distinct point that should strike us about these statistics is they unequivocally demonstrate that the church is following the culture around. To put it bluntly, the world's culture has infiltrated the church. We carry society's mindset around with us since we have never become distinct from the culture around us in: purpose, identity and objectives through conversion and sanctification. Thus, society is influencing the church, not the other way around.

Jesus told us that there would be signs demarcating those whom are His. The Apostle John tells us that "The one who says, 'I have come to know Him,' and does not keep His commandments, is a liar, and the truth is not in him; but whoever keeps His word, in him the love of God has truly been perfected. By this we know that we are in Him," (*cf.* I John 2:4-5). Again, John speaks in his Gospel:

> "Every branch in Me that does not bear fruit, He takes away; and every branch that bears fruit, He prunes it, that it may bear more fruit...I am the vine, you are the branches; he who abides in Me, and I in him, he bears much fruit; for apart from Me you can do nothing. If anyone does not abide in Me, he is thrown away as a branch, and dries up; and they gather them, and cast them into the fire, and they are burned," (*cf.* John 15:2, 5-6).

The Word of God is resolute! Those who *know God* keep His commandments. Additionally, we will bear fruit if we are His, "some a hundredfold, some sixty, and some thirty," (*cf.* Mark 4:20).

Where is the fruit in the church in America?

We cannot say there is none, but we must admit that what we can see is a pittance. In addition, the fruit that we can see is not the same fruit which Christ told us to look for or produce. Jesus never said take dominion over society. Jesus never said try and make a culture outwardly righteous by forcing them to obey a "Judeo-Christian Ethic."

If we were farmers, what would be thought of the "fruit" of our hand if we produced with the scarcity that is evident by the church in this country?

In analyzing the church in America we must realize that we bear a heavy responsibility for Christianity not expanding as fast as the world's population growth. Since America is one of the richest countries and it is said to have the highest concentration of believers, we cannot be absolved of the responsibility for a negative growth rate.

Various numbers are tossed about by scholars and researchers touting the growth of Christianity worldwide. While these are statistical estimations they are based on reliable information which helps to give us a sense of reality. I have gathered some statistical information to help us see what is happening to the Kingdom of God worldwide on a daily basis.

Church Growth -vs.- World Population Growth

The Church			The World	
New Christians[8]	204382	340547	Statistical Birth Rate[9]	
Factored Death Rate*	- 86658	144383 -	Statistical Death Rate[10]	
Approx. Net Growth	117724	196164	Pop. Net Growth[11]	

Divide the Approximate Net Growth Rate by the Population Net Growth and this equals...

World population is growing 58-60 percent faster than the church, i.e. a negative growth!

*Note: The factored death rate is figured at the same percentage as that for the non-christian population.

The figures of Christian growth are somewhat softly rendered since several other negative factors are not figured into this assessment. For further information consult the World Christians Encyclopedia 2nd Ed. Sheet 2 Diagram 3. Pg. 8. You can also check source material at: www.gem-werc.org.

Any measurable growth in the Kingdom is good. However, losing market share, if I can use such a term, is very bad. These statistics can be mulled over in many different ways. But even the best way of parsing them reveals a growth rate that is almost trivial, given the importance of our message, the potential we wield in schooling, monetary backing and political freedom to pursue such activities. We should be taking the world by storm!

So why is missions as slow and as unproductive as it seems to be, given our evangelical mindset and our money? We have all the motivation and resources we need, right?

We cannot even look at evangelism and gloat about the effectiveness of our techniques and endeavors. Barna records that "a majority of people who made a first-time 'decision' for Christ were no longer connected to a Christian church within just 8-weeks of having made such a decision!"[12] This is not preposterous since several other well-known personalities refer to similar details. Ray Comfort in his book, *Hell's Best Kept Secret*, records a 92% failure rate in evangelical campaigns.[13] Both Luis Palau and Billy Graham record up to an 88% "no stick rate" of so-called "decisions for Christ." Bill Faye, the noted evangelist and author of *Share Jesus Without Fear,* once stated on the radio that 85% of church growth is "transfer growth." In other words, local church growth is measured on people hopping from one church to the other instead of being won to Christ. These statistics paint a dismal picture of the church's current condition.

Can we possibly deny what these statistics intimate?

The actual capabilities of the average believer in evangelism work and preparedness is a morass as well. This factor probably reflects some in the low missionary deployment rate in comparison to the financial resources we possess. Speaking of financial resources, one writer states that 80% of the world's Christian finances are in the hands of American Christians.[14] The point of mentioning this statistic is to draw attention to the inconsistencies church people seem to be comfortable with, and to show there is very little intentionality concerning The Great Commission in the organized church. We already have the majority of the world's finances at our disposal, but even if we had all the money in the world we'd still be here politicking to continue enjoying our *deserved wealth* never mind the spiritually dead world outside the USA.

Christians (in America) give less than .033% of their earnings to missions and some say as low as .025%.[15] In comparison, Neil Pirolo writes in his book *Serving as Senders*, "North Americans spend as much on chewing gum as they give to missions."[16] This is unconscionable since we've been given the mandate to disciple the nations and we have the money with which to do it! Remember that supposedly 86% of Americans claim to be Christians. I do not believe this number is anywhere close to being true, but a majority of this 86% claiming to be Christians has got to be in the organized church somewhere at sometime. This claim implicates not some misinformed public but rather what many would call *the church.*

Continuing on our analysis, nine out of ten Americans cannot accurately define the meaning of the "Great Commission."[17] Only 4% of adults polled could not define the "Great Commission" and quote John 3:16 or define "the Gospel."[18] Only 53% of "born-again" Christians feel a sense of personal responsibility to evangelize non-believers.[19] Don't Christians read their Bible? Notice the statistic says that only 53% *feel a sense of responsibility*. This does not indicate that they really ever do anything about it. There is little real emphasis put on personal responsibility for evangelism in most "churches." It has become the *job* of the professional staff of the church instead of believers entering into their priesthood and ministering as scripture tells us, (*cf.* I Pet. 2:9-10). Christ did not instruct only the apostles, e.g. the super-gifted people of "higher-calling," to evangelize the nations. Just before His ascension Christ commanded all present to repeat what He had done with them, (*cf.* Matt. 28:19-20, Luke 24:46-48, Acts 1:7-8). There were more people at his ascension than just the eleven remaining disciples. Thus, Christ was speaking to all believers, even to us.

What about the church's political activities in view of our acclaimed beliefs? In 1999, 40% of Democrats, 54% of Republicans, and 36% of Independents classified themselves as "born-again" Christians.[20] In the same year 40% of "born-again" believers said Bill Clinton was a good example of the Christian faith. All I can say is WOW! Additionally, 48% of "born-again" believers said Clinton was honest and trustworthy.[21] If this country went to war in the past as a nation with people this confused about what is right and wrong, we might be eating rice or waving swastikas, or maybe even enjoying afternoon tea and crumpets.

What could possibly be the cause for all of these negative statistics?

Is this analysis just pessimistic, only looking at the glass half-full?

Other than a negative conclusion, what other analysis should we make of these statistics?

Are we just plain oblivious to the reality that we are out in left field..."asleep in the Light" as Keith Green put it?

The Old Testament gives a picture that has significance to this analysis of our day. Israel made alliances with godless nations around it. The gentiles' ideals and philosophies ended up corrupting Israel, ultimately bringing her down in judgment. We as believers in this country have become so much like the non-believers around us that we cannot possibly do what we have been commanded, (*cf.* Matt. 28:19-20). Could we also be brought down in judgment for having done the same as Israel of old?

The church in America has been in denial for too long! The results of the present approach to: ministry, culture and politics, combined with the denial of failure, will soon reach out and grab us so that many of us won't be able to deny reality any longer. The signs are available for those who want to see. So, why wait to hit the ground at terminal velocity? This society is said to be in a moral free-fall. The chief reason for this reality is that the church is corrupt, walking hand in hand with society. The organized church makes no attempt to offer between the truth of God and the ideals of secular culture because it almost exclusively uses the political stage of the world to do its work. We must wake up, (*cf.* Mal. 3:18).

One of my favorite scriptures is both an encouragement and an exhortation to us at this point.

Hebrews 12:1-8 NASB

Therefore, since we have so great a cloud of witnesses surrounding us, let us also lay aside every encumbrance, and the sin which so easily entangles us, and let us run with endurance the race that is set before us, fixing our eyes on Jesus, the author and perfecter of faith, who for the joy set before Him endured the cross, despising the shame, and has sat down at the right hand of the throne of God. For consider Him who has endured such hostility by sinners against Himself, so that you may not grow weary and lose heart. You have not yet resisted to the point of shedding blood in your striving against sin; and you have forgotten the exhortation which is addressed to you as sons, "*my son, do not regard the discipline of the Lord, nor faint when you are reproved by Him; for those who the Lord loves He also disciplines, and He scourges every son whom He receives.*" It is for discipline that you endure; God deals with you as with sons; for what son is there whom his father does not discipline? But if you are without discipline, of which all have become partakers, then you are illegitimate children and not sons. **(emphasis mine)**

We must throw-off incorrect thinking to embrace our Heavenly calling. We can object to the statistics and their implications or we can admit to ourselves that they are at least representative of the truth and begin down the road that leads back to where we belong. The Holy Spirit will enlighten us as we drop our preconceived ideas and pursue God for God alone no matter the cost. We need to analyze where we have gone off the path. Doing so will help us recover and begin walking as children of light rather than children of the world claiming to be children of light.

THE COZINESS OF
THE CHURCH AND STATE
IS GOOD FOR THE STATE
AND BAD FOR
THE CHURCH

– G.K. Chesterton –

3

Stupid Is As Stupid Does

The title of this chapter was popularized by a line from a comedy-drama movie entitled, *Forrest Gump.* The 1994 movie was a box office smash, grossing in excess of 330 million dollars. This enjoyable story gave a view of life that was not only funny but at some points very poignant. We laugh at different scenes as we ingest and are touched by the directness of its subtle implications. Forrest Gump continuously uses the phrase, "stupid is as stupid does," against his tormenters. While this phrase seems to be a meaning-less retort it is indeed very true, especially when it refers to someone who continues to do the same foolish things over and over. In the course of this chapter we will look at an over-view of the religious conservative's rise to prominence and see the literal junkyard of failed attempts of what is still deemed to be a worthy venture. Some may think this analysis unfair. However, we must see what is true and then reconcile what we think with the realities that our thinking has sired. This may not be comfortable but we must be honest!

The basic idea of the conservative movement even as far back as the early 1960's was to get involved and change the drift of political policy. It was not so much a religious coalition then as it has become today, but the movement was a lightning rod for people of a conservative social bent, to which most deeply religious people could relate. Liberal incrementalism had run a course far enough to the left that conservative type thinkers as well as religious people could not tolerate the trend anymore. So began the polarization to *the right* over issues.

Barry Goldwater was one of the first "conservatives," in our modern view of them, to be taken seriously by the political arena. Goldwater opposed President Eisenhower's huge budget in 1958 as being "too high." In 1960 Goldwater published his conservative ideas in a book, *The Conscience of a Conservative*. With a solid run all the way to the 1964 presidential election, Goldwater gave rise to a segment of the populace inclined to ideas that were different than what either of the two political parties embodied at the time. In retrospect, conservative perspectives had declined steadily through the Eisenhower years and took a nose dive during the early Kennedy/Johnson administration. While there still was decency in the general populace, a dark cloud loomed on the horizon of maturing youth and the American culture as a whole.

Liberals won again in 1964 and so continued the leftward drift. By the time the next Republican was elected in 1968 another near decade came and went of one failed political solution after another. There was so much upheaval in society that it was a wonder war did not break out here in America. Society became so fragmented. The counter-culture became a way for the youth to communicate its ideals to a society that seemed to them hypocritical and out of touch. Thus crouched another division in the political and moral landscape of this country. By the late 60's, Vietnam was all but a total loss. President Lyndon B. Johnson's "Great Society" was in full force eating away at the nation's financial stability. Animosity from the Civil Rights campaign was still being experienced by both sides, while the women's equal rights movement was just burgeoning.

In 1968, Richard Nixon was the man of the hour for conservatives, or so they thought. He was the hope of many. A few years later the character Archie Bunker, on the TV sitcom, *All in the Family*, depicted the hope of simple people for better times and the need for moral footing. To many Nixon was thought to be the man to meet the need. This era presented an epic event in the political arena as well as a continuing destabilization of the young population.

While coming into office, Nixon pandered to the forerunners of what is now known as the Christian Right, courting them into the election. Even Billy Graham was duped into backing Nixon publicly, encouraging people to vote for him in a passive sense by allowing details of his private vote to be known.[1] The conservatives thought their hour had come. Finally, they had a man who could champion their cause. Later, Billy Graham was a little more reserved about supporting a politician after having been embarrassed by the Nixon scandal.[2]

Many Christians were disillusioned by the corruption that embodied the Nixon administration. There was a great sense of betrayal through the whole country for most Americans, even across party lines. Both groups felt that the boondoggle of Watergate was an unconscionable event. Most Americans did not experience the stinging feelings of violation nearly as badly as the conservatives who backed Nixon, putting him into the Oval Office.

By 1973 the Supreme Court's social engineering
decision in the infamous Roe vs. Wade case legalized
abortion. Legalized abortion had finally done it for the
conservatives that were religious, it was too far! Abortion was a moral issue, which all flavors of religious
political conservatives could rally around. Up until
then there was little religious people, on a wide basis,
could agree on much less join hands and fight for.
Now it seemed like the hour of decision for what had
become a broad religious political force. This issue
alone brought about the most prolific attempts at trying to curb a moral plague, but nothing has stopped
the practice. Many a baby has been saved yet the issue
of abortion is still not rectified. Over a three decade
showdown more dust has been raised over this issue
than the issue ever becoming settled itself.

The next chapter, politically speaking, was the
country being led by a *nowhere man* who hung out in
the shadows as the country emotionally processed the
Watergate scandal. Gerald Ford was neither voted for
nor voted against in his 2-1/2 year term. To his credit
he treaded carefully over this delicate time in America,
but the conservative agenda advanced little during this
period.

Next came a Georgian peanut farmer who
claimed to be *born-again*. After the fiasco with Nixon
and the coasting years with Ford, people were looking
for a change. Many conservatives believed this smiling,
gentle Southerner was just the ticket. He was so
mild-mannered and seemed very trustworthy. He was
an affable fellow; however, his combination of faith and
how it affected policy was questionable. He seemed to
be a front man for a power group that had an agenda
and needed someone to put a nice cover over it. Phyllis
Schlafly, known more today for her organization,: *Eagle*

Forum, espoused this theory in her book titled, *A Choice Not an Echo*[3] back in 1964, which sold a whopping 3-million copies.[4] Schlafly referred to an elite group of people putting a specific person in office. She called them "kingmakers."

With regards to Jimmy Carter, nobody could attain that high an office and yet make so many nationally detrimental decisions, unless he was something of a marionette. One thing that Carter did very well was to make being called a "born-again Christian" vogue within the political arena. At the same time he really tarnished what it meant to be a real Christian in a public sense, because he was in over his head and he did such a deplorable job during his administration. Carter became an icon of *political-christianity.*

Still undaunted by the failures of *their men,* by the late 1970's the perennially optimistic conservatives got organized. So convinced about their prospects, convicted about their stand, and driven by continual loss, they truly thought they were capable of winning an election for the top office in the land. And indeed they were! Not only did they think they could win an election, but also control their candidate once in office. They thought they had the president eating out of their hands and that he owed them a lot of big favors because of their support. They had regular access to the White House and a president who also had taken a shine to them. Cal Thomas wrote unflattering correlation between a famous dance couple and the relationship of the Religious-Right with President Regan. "It was said of Fred Astaire and Ginger Rogers that she gave him sex and he gave her class. The Christian conservatives embodied by the Moral Majority gave Ronald Reagan votes, and Ronald Reagan in the White House, gave us credibility."[5]

Well, this shows stupidity. For one thing, the liberals ran aground with Carter and the quagmire he produced. So a conservative Republican win was a great possibility. Secondly, anybody naive enough to think that any real candidate, once elected, would then allow himself to be used as a puppet by a single interest group at the expense of his party is ridiculous. Especially if this group doesn't pose any real threat of retaliation or consequence, should the *would be puppet* get a mind of his own. Politics is a game of manipulation! One must have the tools with which to exert power and force in order to maintain control. In Carter's case, the ones pulling his strings had the money and clout to be of great detrimental consequence.* Conservatives had nothing over Reagan.

Reagan was not like Carter in that he had more control of his political machine. He knew how to hob-nob and network politically. In addition, Reagan had more than just the religious conservatives to placate. So with this win, a trend was institutionalized within the Religious-Right of bellying up to the political hog trough of special interest groups. All, of course, was an attempt to pressure the political arena for support and change. However, conservatives ended up just being used to get in office, to be all but forgotten after Inauguration Day. Ever since Reagan, the Religious-Right has been a force to contend with going into an election, and now political system of America realized it. Now candidates need to bow before this pressure group of "Christians" to gain power.

The story does not end here of course. The Regan years were good from a conservative point of view. This

*Footnote:** This is what has been part of the faulty thinking of conservative Christian political activists. No real Christian can play politically on a national stage because the very nature of politics is compromise and manipulation. These are concepts which Christians should be allergic to, much less be dealing in.

President rebuilt much of the mess Carter had left behind. The Cold War ended just after he left office. Still, under this great leader the conservative agenda was not advanced in any great way. This simply reinforces the idea that the Religious-Right was being taken advantage of just getting who they thought were *"their people"* elected. If the conservative Christians ever had the kind of control they thought they had, more would have been done towards their causes.

It is hard to say what was advanced on the agenda of the conservatives in this period other than staying in the limelight. In all fairness, part of this *non-advancement* was due to the Democrat majorities in both houses, but still the wheels of progress did not move the way they really should have if the conservatives wielded the kind of power they thought they had. The common idea during the high time of the early to mid-80's was *"We've got our man in office and we can ramrod our agenda."* As we know, it did not work out this way. However, the apparent motives and attitudes of the religious conservatives seem plainly demonstrated by their actions. In addition, the error in their approach of top-down culture change through politics seems plainly illustrated by the continual failures of *their men.* The conservative hot potato of abortion was not stopped during this high point of religious conservative political activism. Abortion hasn't been stopped to this day for that matter. Yet, conservatives felt their man Reagan was the champion of their cause, not only on this issue but on many others. The Reagan years were probably the height of religious conservative influence, except for their most recent resurgence. But even the high watermark of the 80's for conservatives was perforated by the misbehaviors of some in the Regan administration.

Not being satisfied by the bone yard of failed conservative attempts to change the downward turn of cultural morality, there came another round of conservative undertaking in the senior Bush years. George H.W. Bush struggled to come off as genuine to the conservatives, he appeared to be *"out of touch* with their perspectives and experience"[6]. Yet the conservative Religious-Right still hung on to Bush as another one of *their men.* The right-wing political activists still took the Republicans' side of the aisle but with less excitement. A real let down came for the religious conservatives in the second half of Bush's administration when he began talking about the "thousand points of light" and the "New-World Order." This is something that any Christian should shudder at having been part of. It is also a further lesson in not putting one's trust in mere men or their princes. In Psalm 146:3 God tells us, "Do not trust in princes, in mortal man, in whom there is no salvation." Many religious people refused to believe Bush's rhetoric and its implications to be what it really was. So many could not believe that what was being implied by the elder Bush was in fact *one-world government.* Even though conservatives were not excited about this guy, he was still one of *their men* and he was promoting this idea? Unbelievable!

Then came the Clinton years. Whew! People disillusioned by moderate prosperity and with a sense of complacency, feeling a sense of betrayal over "read my lips, no new taxes...," fell in love with a self invented "new" Democrat who had a bit of glamour and charisma. Bill Clinton's election confounded the Religious-Right, so they went to work to put the controls on this bad boy from Arkansas. The Religious-Right had gotten a little soft in the mid to late 80's, but Bill Clinton gave them a real sense of urgency.

By 1994 the Republicans, with the help of the religious conservatives, put together a remarkable deal for the American voters called, *The Contract With America.* The Republicans intended to accomplish several objectives within 100-days of gaining office, provided they could capture a majority in the Congress. The Republicans succeeded in gaining their majority. They even pushed through several little items of legislation which had been promised. However, barely anything else came from this group of new recruits. Most accomplishments were only marginal details morally speaking, meanwhile the underlying issues formulating the Religious-Right's platform continued to go untouched. Once again, this gives evidence of the naiveté of conservative Christians in their belief that they could reestablish cultural morality through politics.

Even in this resurgence of power the religious conservatives continued to hold the hands of the Republican Party, which seemed virtually impotent against the insanity of the moral free-fall that President Clinton embodied. In those years Rush Limbaugh, the recently self sullied talk show host, continually ranted about the seeming impotency of this majority. The Religious-Right had invested the advancement of its interests with the Republican Party and for the first time in 40-years the Republicans had won a majority in both Houses. Yet at this pinnacle none of the real core issues that defined the movement were advanced in a legislative sense.[7] Certainly there was more *awareness* about their issues but this is not what the movement was about.

The movement was about moral change, yet never has the imagined abortion amendment come up in session. Never has school prayer been reestablished, as if that really matters for any true believer anyway.

The "sanctity of life" is a banner that many politicians walk under; so far they only seem to give lip service to it. The "homosexual agenda" has not been stemmed. Conservatives having a hand in the top executive office in the land has not turned out to be the political savior they had imagined it would be. Only in the younger Bush's era has a ban on expanding fetal tissue research been accomplished and on governmentally subsidized partial birth abortions have been stopped. This ban on federally funded fetal tissue research does nothing to stop privately funded work. So what is the difference? All this *progress* is minuscule compared to the time, effort and money flushed down the toilet of the cultural manipulation game in trying to achieve these paltry gains!

While the younger Bush is not failing badly on moral fronts, but no one can declare success yet. In his second term Bush seems a bit more aloof on *moral issues*. While the younger Bush seems to be a devout man, at the same time he is making more decisions that appeal to the "moderate." George W. Bush is making many decisions that continue to advance *globalism* and the *New-World Order* his father announced. He miscued when he to referenced Islam a *"peaceful religion"* saying that Moslems worship the same God as the Christians do. Bush's comment is pure unadulterated *interfaithism,** a new unseen hazard for simple minded church people. The younger Bush seems to be the closest to success conservatives can point to in 40-years of effort, even then Bush is bittersweet.

Footnote: "Interfaithism" is a word coined to express the combining of normally dissimilar beliefs, i.e. Islam, Jewish and Buddhist along with other religious/ philosophical groups into a hybrid religion. In order to have a "one-world government" a "one-world religion" will have to come into prominence. Author Gary Kah has documented this direction at the UN all the way back into the 1950's, You can access his material at: www.garykah.org

The conservative right was squarely behind George W. Bush all the way through the election of his second term. Yet immediately the day after, they had to go to work to make sure their issues were protected from other Republican Party members like Arlan Spector. Spector, a liberal Republican (a.k.a. a moderate), who could likely be named to chair the judiciary committee, has threatened early to derail any attempt by Bush to nominate conservative judges to the Supreme Court. Conservatives will not be happy with Bush in the long run, because he is not the conservative they think he is and he will continue his moderate positions in favor of a legacy.

Thus, we have a broad picture of the last 40 or so years of the conservative religious political saga in whatever form it has taken. In short, they have earnestly struggled to attain political power or to attach themselves to those who are politically powerful in order to try and effect change. All conservatives have successfully accomplished in 40-years is putting all their fingers in the increasing number of holes in a dam that is still disintegrating. This is tantamount to polishing the brass railings on a Titanic that has already been slit open by an iceberg. It's a sad commentary. If we believe this approach we are reduced to merely reacting to the latest *flavor of the week* moral emergency cooked up for us. This kind of political involvement both disenfranchises and distracts the followers of Christ from their true calling.

What would lead a group of intelligent people with a supposed "biblical" focus to go down such a reckless and unproductive path as political manipulation to accomplish moral purposes?

We will find some answers in the following chapters.

LIVING IS EASY
WITH EYES CLOSED,
MISUNDERSTANDING
ALL YOU SEE...

– John Lennon –
From: Strawberry Fields Forever

4

How Did We Get Here, Anyway?

There is an old saying: the quickest way to the wrong place is to start out in the wrong direction. Given the lackluster track record of the religious conservative movement in its 40-years concerted effort, we probably should begin to seriously question the activist's approach. Because of the unexplainable* failures of conservative activists over these many years it seems plausible to submit that God likely did not purpose for the church to pursue political control *en masse* as a real means to change society. God is not into failure and futility; these are marks of mankind's best efforts in the flesh. We must conclude that Christians, who are unquestionably sincere in their political activism, must have started out in the wrong direction in the first place. Either that or we need to redefine futility and failure.

So, "How did we get here, anyway"?

*Footnote: "Unexplainable" meaning there is no rational reason, from the conservative's mindset, for the failure to succeed in turning public policy to a morally correct position during the past 40-years. Cases in point: abortion, and the homosexual agenda. Some may still deny any failure, pointing instead to various minor successes, e.g. the ban on Partial Birth Abortion. To deny mass failure and then justify it by incidental stop gaps is the way to continue in futility and to be occupied with a farce rather than God's objectives.

What has brought the church in America to the point of jumping into the hog trough of politics en masse?

The answer to these questions will help define the precipitative factors leading the church in the direction of political activism as the chief means of changing culture and supposedly doing our work on the earth. It does not seem that people of their own natural mind delude themselves in order to go about living their lives, yet scores of people knowingly impose ignorance upon themselves. In addition, many well educated believers refuse to expose themselves to ideas that are new to them,* apparently because they don't want to bother struggling through to find truth. Truth, of course, doesn't grow on trees.

Society wants three easy steps to freedom in life or some other such effortless personal improvement program. The church in large part has contracted this *Burger King* syndrome: "you can have it your way," which is laden with the immediacy of instant gratification. The conservative movement in similar step has also become, a reactionary quick fix mindset, based on society's tendencies. This is a tremendous problem because people of faith willingly operate under various pretenses they do not fully understand and may not agree with if they took the effort to think about it. Either we are doing activities in life because we know what we believe and why we believe it, or we are being dominated/used by what others believe and why they believe it. Since there is a rush to have what we want immediately (culture change) we've ingested the approach of worldly philosophy as a means to our end. We have been unwilling to sift through what they offer us, differentiating the diluting preoccupations that appear to be spiritual from real spiritual truth.

---

*Footnote: We discussed this concept of ideas not being *new*, just maybe *new to us* in Chapter 1, *Subjective Thinking In The Camp*, page 23.

The intelligence community tells us that people become weakened in their conviction by an acute personal desire or some area of intense inner imbalance. These hidden details can cause people to lose their objectivity. Anybody with these kinds of underlying problems will look for the one thing, settle for something else entirely accepting the fraud as the object of their intent in the first place. What they've settled for is expedient to the deeper driving forces in their life, not their verbally acclaimed beliefs. Paul gives us an illustration of this tendency in his Epistle to the church in Rome.

Romans 1:21-25 NASB

"For even though they knew God, they did not honor Him as God, or give thanks; *but they became futile in their speculations, and their foolish heart was darkened. Professing to be wise, they became fools, and exchanged the glory of the incorruptible* God for an image in the form of corruptible man and of birds and four-footed animals and crawling creatures. Therefore God gave them over in the lusts of their hearts to impurity, that their bodies might be dishonored among them. *For they exchanged the truth of God for a lie, and worshiped and served the creature rather than the Creator*, who is blessed forever. Amen.

The people Paul referred to in this text wanted to be wise, but because of various underlying factors they accepted foolishness instead. Their *underlying issues* became the impetus for accepting foolishness and operating under it as if it were truly wise. Overriding desires and imbalances became a catalyst to accept things which are less than optimum. This detail is an important clue in identifying the problems behind the church's affinity with politics as a means of morally perfecting the culture of this country. The church also wants to be wise but because of our *underlying issues* we have accepted the fraud, of *changing society's exterior morality* through the constraints of the legislative process in an attempt to amend the constitution, while leaving the meaty issue of people's relationship with God untouched in the process. And many spiritual leaders sincerely believe we have done what God want us to do. We've accepted foolishness as wisdom and have been failing ever since.

There are three fundamental elements that form the foundation underneath the church's deviation into politics as a means of doing what we think God wants. Perhaps there are other factors, but few are as foundational to the church's forays into the political arena than the short list below. These elements are the church's imbalances and overriding desires.

These Elements Are:
1. A subjective view of history.
2. A focus on theology over a relationship with God.
3. An incorrect perception of identity.

For followers of Christ the picture of who and what we are should flow completely from what the written word of God says and what God is telling us today on a personal basis. It seems reasonable to say many people base their beliefs not so much on the Bible as they do on theology.* Theological thinking is based on scripture but it is not scripture itself. If the common church person cannot understand basic teachings of scripture, or quote what used to be commonly known texts of scripture, it does not seem that the average churchgoer, who is a religious political activist, can understand the theological underpinnings for what they are doing in their *activism*. It has been my experience

*Footnote:** We will show evidence of this heavy reliance on theology by the institutional church beginning on page 66.

that most politically active Christians are only able to parrot a few theological statements or some badly hatched texts, which might seem to support these theological views and actions towards political activism. Notice the order of focus, theology first and scripture second. This should scare us tremendously!

Over the years I've sent letters to various national ministries seeking deeper answers on what the scriptural support is for our politics and our ideas of citizenship/patriotism. I wanted to try and disprove my thesis that there is actually very little scripture that could be taken to support the political and patriotic views of the modern day church. I felt the best way to learn why the church has adopted its view on political activity was to listen to the people many other people listen to. Perhaps these ministers had greater insight and wisdom than just a pastor, some local Bible teacher or a layman. Sadly, about ninety-five percent of the responses came back in pure theological terminology, not scriptural support or denunciation. It is frightening to me to think that many of the beliefs in the organized church are based more on the evolutions of theology than scripture.

I spoke to one apologist from Canada about Christians dominating politics, after he had given a class at a missionary school about the need for Christians to *"take ground"* in society through politics. His concepts and terminology* reminded me of certain theological mindsets I had read about, which are bent on dominating the political arena for moral purposes. Yet, the apologist did not recognize the correlation between his concepts and the polemic lingo used by certain proponents of this politically dominating theology we shall discuss the next chapter. I would say the two were no different, except that the teacher didn't re-

*Footnote: Specific terms or catch phrases often identify specific groups of people e.g., "Once Saved Always Saved," or "do you have the 'anointing?" We can generally identify people's theological leaning by the terminology they use.

alize what he was really teaching was the same thing as those who think the Christian's singular job is to reconstruct society in the model of the Old Testament (OT) law system.

There are various theological positions which support political activism but scripture tends to be on the short end of the support basis. To illustrate, one recent well-known book alleges *a scriptural mandate* for Christians to be politically active. Of the 72-texts used in this 190-page book, only 9 verses directly support the thesis of this so-called mandate. The other 63-texts were either twisted, misused or were merely ancillary to some other aspects of the book. Conservatives will find it very difficult to use the entire Bible to support their view of political domination. They do well with just a few texts. As mentioned in other chapters, recent historical events play the important role of "proof text" for the activist more than scripture. The author's mindset, on the above mentioned book, shows this same tendency. Similarly, many everyday people I know, who advocate the political activist mindset use only a few scriptural texts in support of their political affinities. There are great amounts of scripture dealing with how we ought to relate to the society and the state around us, which point to a totally different approach.

Only one of the various national radio ministries I contacted came up with a more biblically plausible answer for the modern approach to the church/state debate than is commonly available. It is scary to me that solid answers, on such a high impact subject, are so hard to come by, especially when people look to these ministry sources with the expectation of getting solid answers. How many times have we all heard an acquaintance tout some well-known minister on a thought or two? "Dr. So-and-So said such-and-such on his show last week?" This is not wrong, but if we cannot source our conviction directly in the Bible alone, then we are depending too much on man's ideas. This is dangerous ground since none of these men will stand with us before God to answer for our actions.

We dare not condemn an idea just because we have spoken to a few radio ministries, or an apologist or an author about incongruities of a view with the Bible. In the case of church/state relations we are not talking about some small offshoot idea with which few are involved. There are hundreds of positional treatises on church/state relations from almost every type of religious thinker. And I can tell you first hand that the majority opinion in church circles today is supportive of active political involvement, either from the left or right.* If the average Christians cannot articulate basic scriptural foundations for what they do,[1] and if they cannot understand the verbal content of the most commonly used version of the Bible in this country,[2] it shouldn't take a rocket scientist to determine that the theological concepts behind all the church/state debate is well beyond common folk in church. Few today are attempting to question the ramifications of the ideas of the Religious-Right. Thus, most church people are gleefully operating on theological ideas they don't really understand. That is dangerous!

The average church person has greater aversion to taking prescription medicine they're not familiar with, than employing theologies with which they are just as unfamiliar. One should not make an investment, mental or financial, without researching to see if investing is really warranted. We have been warned about giving to "charities" because there are so many scams taking peoples' earnest giving and using it in ways other than for what it was intended. Why don't we look as carefully at what is presented to us in our *thought investments* and "beliefs"?

Footnote: By active political involvement I mean, *en masse* domination or manipulation of politics or parties for a moral end, especially when we have little else to do with society other than living in it and profiting from it.

Who can say that the ideals various religious groups offer are legitimate in an absolute sense? Only the Word of God can judge the thoughts and intentions of anybody's heart or the ideas that are constantly bandied about today. We need to go back to scripture! In the meantime, we will begin to dissect each element of the foundation for the church's deviation, which has directed religious conservatives by the droves into their political forays as practically their only means of changing the culture. Fundamental/Evangelical and Charismatic types would be quick to deny the reality of a one sided game plan. However, they have little else to do with the secular, non-christian society around them other than grandstanding their political/moral views and then trying to cram these down society's throat through the political process. Anybody who can't see that this is happening isn't using any sense of perception.

5

Theology As A Motivator For Political Activism

Theology is touted to be the study of God. The Greek word "theo" means God. The suffix, "ology" means the study of a specific matter delineated by the prefix. This word is a misnomer from the beginning. Anytime finite people try to study an infinite God and articulate what they find, there will be insurmountable problems in the process. In reality theology is more of an interpretive philosophical approach to studying what is knowable about God than a means of actually coming to know God in a deeper way. Since theology is the device of men, it is fraught with problems—one of which is the continuous evolution of ideas. In this chapter we will see partly why theology has become one of the preeminent components on which the machine of political activism operates.

In our day, theology plays a king's role in the organization and practice of the average institutional church. Much of our talk about beliefs are couched in strictly theological terminology. At any church building you can find a "statement of faith," which defines that group. In every statement I have ever looked at, the majority of points are pitched along theological lines.

There is a cornucopia of beliefs one may find at one place or another. For example: Eternal Security or Free Will, types of Millennialism, modes of baptism, the operation of the gifts of the Spirit or the cessation of these gifts at some point in history, etc.

The basic premise of most theology is of course the desire to acquire a higher purpose or greater purity in belief. This *could be exemplary* except this was also the endeavor of the Pharisees in Jesus' day. While the Pharisees' motive was good in what they intended to do Jesus condemned them for their hypocrisy and their invention and practice of traditions nullifying the commands of God. There is a hint of arrogance in theology, which a fellow of the 17th Century delightfully illustrates for us. He wrote,

> The great number of teachers is the reason for the multitude of sects, for which we shall soon have no more names. Each church reckons itself as the true one, or at least the purest, truest part of it, while among themselves they persecute each other with the bitterest of hatred... Out of the Bible they forge their different creeds; these are their fortresses and bulwarks behind which they entrench themselves to resist all attacks.[1]

In keeping with the inventions of the Pharisees there is one particular theological school of thought that is of great consequence to our discussion of politics in the church and that is *Reformed Theology*. This system of thought has existed in various forms since the time of Martin Luther. One of its early champions was John Calvin. Calvin in many ways was similar to today's latest derivatives in Reformed Theology which has been an identifiable grouping for only 50-years or so. We can call them *"Dominionists"* at this point as a general designation (this term will be explained in greater detail). In any case, the main difference between Calvin and today's Dominionist is that this modern nuance has mixed a popular retelling of history with their theological mindset. This combination of a self-aggrandizing history, religious philosophy [ergo theology], combined with a third component of a mistaken identity, makes for a strong cord that grips a large degree of the church population in this country.

This modern form of Reformed Theology has four sub-groups of thought that some outsiders see as being one think-tank. The overviews given in the following pages are simplified for purposes of brevity. Proponents of these views may disagree with these synopses simply because they are too brief to represent the *full* intellectual depth embodied in their voluminous and nuanced positional treatise work.

Let us be reminded that God in all His wisdom has reduced what we need to know to get to know Him to a single small book. It can be taught to the simplest of children and can be carried in a shirt pocket. This should be a warning to people who approach a belief in God through their vast intellectual positions. It is also a warning to us not to walk in these ways ourselves.

Here are brief overviews of four schools of thought within modern Reformed Theology.

Dominion Theology is based on a strong integration of the OT interpretations into Christian living applications. This view stems from the scripture in Genesis 1:28 where God tells man to take "dominion" over the earth. It is carried through the Law of the OT into the NT wherein *"dominion"* is equated to spreading of the Gospel by taking dominion over every aspect of life and existence in the secular world, bringing each under the "Lordship" of Jesus Christ. Strong critics see this as "Christian Totalitarianism." Promoters view it as a pure practice of Christ's work in this world.

Kingdom Theology is similar to Dominion Theology. However, it emanates from another theological stand having to do with end-times viewpoints (eschatology). Proponents believe that Christians will create a Kingdom for Christ to come back and reign over. Many of them believe in *"Post-millennialism,"* the idea that Christ will return after a 1000-year period of peace and prosperity *that they have achieved*. They believe that human existence is getting better and will culminate in Christ's Kingdom. They believe that there is a long future ahead of us and Christ's return is not imminent.

Theonomy focuses on the Biblical Law. This view holds that all laws recorded in the first five books of the OT (Pentateuch) are binding on all peoples of all nations everywhere and forever. This would exclude laws abolished by Jesus in the NT such as dietary, sabbatical laws or ceremonial laws. Theonomists believe that governments are obligated to keep and govern by God's law. There is common ground between Theonomy and Dominion Theology as far as forcing everyone in society to comply regardless of one's own private beliefs. Exerting power to achieve these goals would be obtained through government and/or authority given to a Theonomic believer by the current governing authority structures.

Reconstructionism is a theological stand that proposes the idea that society, especially that of the United States, is morally and culturally degenerate and must be "reconstructed" according to OT biblical standards. There is a belief amongst these people that America is a covenant nation, meaning America is supposedly chosen by God over all the other nations and set apart for His special purpose just as Israel was in the OT. This approach also has strains of Dominion Theology mixed in with it. Some critics have described the view of *Reconstructionism* as a virulently political theology.

Just below I have provided websites that are either critical, neutral, or promoting these views. I want to be fair and honest with their material. I think you should have the opportunity to see various perspectives on these same points for yourself so that I am not misinterpreting their ideas.

But for us common folk, what's the difference in these positions? Some use these terms interchangeably, which is yet another stumbling block in dealing with theology. One of the greatest dangers concerning this kind of religious philosophy is that it oversteps the simplicity Christ expressed in His gospel. Paul warns against this very thing in II Corinthians 11:3 "But I fear, lest by any means, as the serpent beguiled Eve by his subtlety, so your minds should be corrupted from the simplicity that is in Christ" (NKJV). The second danger about these views is that they put a thrust behind believers to do and be things which Christ *NEVER* advocated or gave example of in His life or work. If we are not following Christ's example, then who are we following?

Even with the negative aspects of theology's continual evolution, it is both interesting and puzzling

Footnote: These four forms of theology are seen by some as the same, even though there are differences between them. I have gathered a few websites which can give a sampling of information about these particular systems of thought. Each site may have mention of the other three systems.

Dominion Theology:
    http://www.rapidnet.com/~jbeard/bdm/Psychology/cor/dominion.htm
    http://www.biblicist.org/bible/dominion.htm
    http://www.equip.org/free/CP0606.htm

Kingdom Theology:
    http://members.tripod.com/thecontenders/kingdom1.htm
    *there are additional pages to this one.

Cont'd on the bottom of the next page

how theological stands that identify one group bleed back into groups that are predecessory in their order of development. One would think that the evolution of thought would be lineally progressive instead of back feeding through older groupings from time to time.

One school of thought, thinking themselves to be the most orthodox form of Christianity seen today, are Fundamentalist/Evangelical traditions having roots in pre-American Reformed Theology. Fundamentalism is much different from Dominionism in that it focuses mainly on the basics of what is necessary to be a Christian. Dominionism is more focused on *taking ground in society* and controlling it for God as a means of being a light and a force for righteousness, i.e. the Dominionist's rendition of evangelism. But the two come together under politics holding each others' hand, tag teaming secular society.

This compilation between Fundamental Evangelicalism and Dominionism is an odd mix. It is perhaps a rediscovery of the approach behind Calvin's Geneva. Calvin "reformed" Geneva where he developed rigid codes of regulation for the church and state. Though never elected nor even a citizen, Geneva felt the heavy hand of this reformer who had a hand in burning heretics and eliminating dissenters from his concoction of neo-Phariseeism. Calvin was forced to leave Geneva after a while simply because of his approach. There is only so far that secular people will go along with pushy religious fundamentalism, like that of Calvin. Calvin

Theonomy:
> http://www.forerunner.com//theofaq.html
> http://pages.quicksilver.net.nz/theonomy/whatis.html

Reconstructionism:
> http://www.serve.com/thibodep/cr/rc.htm
> http://religiousmovements.lib.virginia.edu/nrms/ChRecon.html
> http://www.serve.com/thibodep/cr/whatis.htm
> http://www.crownrights.com/reconstruction/

General Reference:
> http://www.religioustolerance.org/reconstr.htm

did eventually came back to Geneva his example of cultural domination was never one which Christ advocated, nor should we.

Another interesting point about theology is that groups which follow any specific school of thought tends to be very provincial, meaning they stay to themselves. Groups professing differing views do not cross the lines that define the differences between groups. For example, you will not find teachers of Prosperity Theology speaking to groupings of the Plymouth Brethren or the Amish... However, there seems to be some transfer of newer thought into older groups regarding the church and politics. To see evidence of this, let's look at the late Bill Bright. Mr. Bright, the founder of Campus Crusade for Christ, was one of the best-known modern evangelical types in this country. Yet, at one point he took on the approach of the Dominionist, i.e. a more recent school of thought regarding government, society and the Christian. In the foreword of a book called, *Save America*, Mr. Bright wrote:

> "*We Christians must get involved in politics and government as an act of obedience to the Lord.* God's servants have been admonished *to subdue the Earth, (cp. Gen. 1:28).* We are not to be passive spectators: we are called to be involved in the action. First Century Christians were world changers for Christ. *Whether or not we become involved in the affairs of our nation at this critical moment in history will in my judgment, determine life or death for America.*"[2] **(Emphasis Mine)**

This quotation shows just one example of the modern mutation of theology that adopts progressions of ideas which identify groups that are not normally connected. While we consider what Bright had to say in a theological comparison, we also ought to question if there really are scriptures mandating our obedience to God in the specific way of being involved in politics as Bright suggests. There are *NO* such texts which can be construed the way Mr. Bright suggested. Maybe there is an elusive *missing link* in scripture that allows for theologians to make such wild interpretations. Or maybe theologians are using what we could call *artistic license* in interpreting scriptures' meaning. Additionally, Bright's interpretation of the 1st Century believers as "world changers" is a bit twisted from the truth. The 1st Century believers did not go about their lives/work to change the world; it was changed because of their Kingdom work. Culture change was the by-product not the objective.

Bill Bright never changed his thinking in support of the church pursuing the political arena as evidenced by his recent support for books in the genre Dominionist thinking just prior to his death. Bill Bright is not the only mainstream evangelical to adopt residues of the Dominionists' mindset. Today many popular Christian radio personalities use the same demagogic terminology as Dominion Theology proponents use in their approach to politics. It seems that most evangelicals make this adoption without realizing any connection or any problem. You can identify these people by their stance of trying to keep politics as the main field of conquest for the church. Their rhetoric is synonymous with Dominion teaching.

Now that it has been demonstrated that ideas bleed backward through their order of development we should ask a very important question. *Why?* There must be some other common ground between the various groups which allows the thought of successors to bleed back into the former. Sin is common to all people but I don't think that is the key in this case. The only other plausible items that would be common ground between these groups would be a view of history and a perceived identity. Evidence of both of these aspects, history and perceived identity, remarkably turn up in the views of various groups who are definitely not "Dominionist" in the specific sense of the definition. Yet these Evangelical/Fundamental types and even Charismatics, that normally have nothing to do with one another, have adopted this modern notion of the Dominionists in their worldviews to the degree that it is definable in their positions and in the way they articulate their political motives. Other than the aspects of identity and a common view of history that all groups ascribe to, there are no other elements as applicably consistent between the groups within Calvinistic, Evangelical, Fundamentalist or even Charismatic orientations.

This leads us to the next facet in our trilogy discussion of motivations for political conquest by conservatives in the church. Our view of "history" has a large role in the way we look at life and existence as we shall see.

I HAVE BEEN "DOING" HISTORY
FOR NEARLY FORTY YEARS
AND I KNOW HOW
INDECISIVE AND
HOW NONDEFINITIVE..
AND FLIMSY IS ANY
PHILOSOPHY OR THEOLOGY
WHICH IS BASED ON THOSE
RESULTS.
IT IS SAND UPON SAND.

– Jacques Ellul –

6

History As A Motivator For Political Activism

History is a very complex study. Yet, I wonder if church people make more of it than is really necessary. It is the goal of this chapter to scrutinize commonly held ideas about recent history and find out whether they are as needed or correct as is commonly thought. In addition, we will discover how our views of history can motivate us in ways that are not in keeping with who we really are and what our intended purposes should be as followers of Christ.

It is said that there is much to learn from history. We are commonly told if we don't know history we can't really understand where we are today. History is meant to answer many of the "why(s)" about the past as well as providing us a path to our current situation. Another thought commonly quoted about history states: "If you don't learn from history you are condemned to repeat it."

While these common ideas about history contain bits of truth for the natural unconverted man, what about for the follower of Christ?

We touched on the concept of "formative imprinting" in Chapter 1, *Subjective Thinking In The Camp.*

Now we will further develop this idea and show how it can make us partially defective as believers. We grow up in a secular world that educates us, putting a great emphasis on history. When we come into Christ, our identity and significance take on an entirely new origin. Many Christians still lean on the history they were taught as young secularists, even after they are "converted." This unequal yoking stunts our growth in Christ. The formative imprinting of our childhood education in history is never challenged by the reality of being a new creation in Christ as the Bible teaches. One text that comes to mind is, "Old things are passed away, behold *ALL* things are become new," (*cf.* II Cor. 5:17 KJV). This text is taught, rarely if ever, regarding our former secular identity as being part of the "old things are passing away." The imprinting of a national identity and belonging that history gives us is never dissolved. It is then difficult to live out the truth of our new identity because an exchange between "old and new" is not offered, facilitated or required in modern teachings of what it means to be converted and follow Christ. Thus, we must look at this detail of history's importance again to gain God's perspective.

The Problem With History

Obtaining a truly accurate understanding of history can become a life-long study due to the sheer volume of information. With the vastness of historical data we can become tempted to settle on an outlook that simply gives us significance rather than seeking what a comprehensive understanding might give us. Accepting a view does not necessarily mean one perspective or another is truly correct. It might only mean that the outlook we've settled on gives us the greatest sense of comfort in our lives and existence. After all, isn't that what we've been taught to expect from history?

These *deeper issues* concerning history can skew our understanding of what God wants for His church over the course of human existence. History can become a wedge that drives divisions into a group of people where no division exists from God's perspective. History has a mysterious power that manipulates those who are attached to it in the way of having identity, belonging or purpose. It is important that we distinguish the difference between history as man sees it and God's assessment of human events, "There is nothing new under the sun." God's perspective is a single source that can fit in a shirt pocket. Any other source must be at the bottom of the list of what might have sway on us as followers of Christ.

If we are following God, shouldn't we agree with God's perspective?

For the follower of Christ, the history of man can only be the story of the rise and fall of one nation after another. If believers try to make more of history than this, we end up with something that becomes either self-serving and manipulative or at least very problematic in supporting who and what we really are as followers of Christ.

One of the greatest obstacles of using history as a means of thinking about ourselves as followers of Christ is that we are faced with determining which rendition of history is objectively true. There are a number of views covering each era, all claiming to be "history." Some views even contradict one another. If we are going to allow ourselves to base motive or significance in history we cannot ignore any of these various perspectives if they are based on facts. Nor can we divorce the factual realities in these views from the perspective we choose to believe. As we can see, using history can quickly become another quagmire for the believer, just like theology.

Which View Of History Is Right?

To illustrate the evidence that there are differing vantage points on the same section of history, let's look at the founding of America. We will see that most people cling to one view or another out of self-serving motives rather than finding and standing on absolute truth. Let's start with the current undertow of thought in the public education system and then compare it to other viewpoints concerning this same section of history.

Conservatives judge the public school's rendition of American history to be *revisionistic.* This word describes the purposed removal of certain bits of information that do not support a presupposed theory or philosophy employed to analyze any certain era. In plain words, Christians accuse secularists in the education system of systematically eliminating all references to God or Christianity which naturally occurred in American History. Since many of the educational elite do not believe in God, they don't want others to see His hand in any historical affair and be tempted to believe in Him. In an effort to carry out their agenda, they simply delete historical accounts referencing God or Christianity's influence in the events of this country. The conservatives are reasonably accurate in their concerns and analysis of what is happening in the public education system. The conservatives' assessment points out just one example of an outlook on history: the secularists'.

Now, can we learn from this rendition of history? Not really; this view is inaccurate. It has been purposely twisted and is therefore unreliable.

Now that we have perspective on the secularist view, let's look at conservative Christians themselves to see how they fare at an accurate telling of American's founding. A small group within the conservative

Christian populace reacted to the public school system squelching God out of the picture in the historical accounts of this country's founding. In turn they have gathered a telling of their own about this period to reassert "the truth." Their rendition of America's origin is termed *providential.* Providential, meaning that events of the founding were controlled and/or orchestrated for God's divine purpose.

In the 1970's there was one book published which sparked unprecedented interest in this perspective, entitled *The Light and The Glory.** This book is a fanciful reinterpretation of many real historical events. Various details, which support the providential view, were strung together and reinterpreted by the authors as being purely providential. This book is devoid of many facts that would otherwise deflate the theoretic position that America was ever a "Christian-Nation." The authors blatantly gloss over many other facts to arrive at their conclusion that America was a special nation of destiny in God's economy, a "covenant nation" as some term it. The evidence of this "stretch" in interpretation is obvious as one author states, "Another political dead-end [spiritual too] for believers *is the effort to turn the United States into a self-avowed Christian Republic"*[1] (i.e. a Christian-Nation).

Can we really learn from this view of history? Not really.

Footnote: These sincere authors are impossible to believe. There are documentable facts that contradict their assessment of God's purposed effort in America's founding. If these other facts had been considered in conjunction with what they said was "providential" it would cause serious doubt about the conclusions that this country was God's special place, as it was depicted in this book. These authors' work is not an accurate telling of history, just a very partial one. We cannot divorce all the realities while recounting an era of history and still call it correct. What is godly about rebellion, slavery, the treatment of Indians, Freemasonry, Unitarianism, Deism and Enlightenment thinking, which are all intrinsically part of the fabric of this country's founding? Where in the Bible do you find the ideas of "life, liberty and the pursuit of happiness?" Why was this country in such need of the Second Great-Awakening if this country was a *Christian-Nation,* as the authors suggest? The authors' theological ideas taint the way they've chosen to look at and reinterpret this part of history.

This retelling is merely a fantastically unrealistic interpretation: a self-serving paraphrase. It is very inaccurate. Additionally, this view has the effect on its readership of motivating them to see this country as specifically theirs, and God's, both of which cannot be substantiated biblically. Another affect is that this perspective abrogates truths in the Bible, one specifically is that the physical nation of Israel was the only "covenant-nation" God instituted/

In addition, the slant of the providentialist comes dangerously close to certain Mormon teachings about America. This detail alone has caused me to question the validity of the providential view. Politically conservative believers that allow themselves to subscribe to this particular retelling of history are nothing more than pots calling the kettle black. Without realizing it, they have become just as revisionistic as their arch-nemesis "the liberal public education system."

To add confusion to the mix, there is yet a third perspective with a different approach to history than the first two. The *"conspiratorial"* view contends that history is being engineered or purposely designed by certain entities or power groups rather than being accidental or providential as the other two perspectives espouse. Conspiratorialists believe that there are "dark forces" at work behind the scenes, at all levels of government, education, entertainment and media, seeking to subject the world and its population to a one-world government. They have support to look at history in this fashion and they have published reams of facts and documentation over the years.

So, can we really learn from this view of history?

Not really. This view is known to be questionable in its assumptions and is therefore unreliable. The conspiracy theories create a paranoia and build an unnatural suspicion in its readership. Conspiratorialism questions the scriptural teaching that Christ has overcome the world. Believers should not be afraid and always suspicious. Most conspiracies are not as pervasive as many conspiratorialist would like to make it appear. Certainly, there is conspiracy within the human realm. Yet it is no stretch biblically speaking to say that conspiracy is also a device of the enemy of our souls. It is just as plausible to believe that the enemy and his minions orchestrate much of what the conspiratorialist interpret to be a strictly humanly devised affair on the physical level.

What have we learned about different views of history?

We must conclude that any of these views cannot be accepted exclusively and still be considered accurate. These views are limited to, and interpreted by presupposed ideas. We can also see that perspectives are accepted not so much because they are true as much as that they fit the perspective of supporting an agenda. For example: the secularists say there is no God, and in deceit they try to erase any reference to Him in the public arena to help further their agenda of anti-belief. Many Christians say that America is a "Christian-Nation," because this is what they want to believe. They overlook or downplay much that would otherwise overturn their theory. The conspiratorialist looks at every event as if some "clandestine group" is behind everything that happens, again because they want to. In turn they look at every event for the potential to buttress their theory and to warn against the inevitable gloom and doom.

In other words, each group looks at history through a set of glasses. Then they interpret everything in light of the perspective correction of their view or agenda. They do not allow other information to be considered which might challenge the premise they use to qualify the value of historical events. This is a problem if we as followers of Christ are to take history seriously and base our worldview on what we have extracted from our study of historical events.

Before we continue let me further buttress my contention that differing views of history heavily impact and motivate their adherents, through another means. A fellow named Comenius, a 17th Century bishop, educator, and philosopher, beautifully illustrates my point in the form of allegory. He wrote:

> Then we came to another square where I observed something new. Not a few people stood here with certain crooked and curved pipes, one end of which they pressed to their eyes, and the other they placed over their shoulder facing backwards. When I inquired... the interpreter explained that they were telescopes with which one could see behind one's back, [i.e. history]... I begged one of them [who were using such "telescopes"] to lend me his so that I could see through it.... Through each one I saw things *differently*. Through one an object seemed far away, while through another the same thing seemed nearer. Through one telescope something appeared one color, through another, a different color; and a third, it disappeared altogether. Thus I determined that one could not be certain that things were as they appeared; rather the color a thing appeared depended on how the telescope was positioned. *From this I perceived that each one believed his own perspective.*[2]

This insightful quote illustrates that others are well aware that various points of view on history can twist our perception to where objectivity and reality are impossible. We cannot dismiss this problem regarding believers who continue to look at American History from perspectives other than simply: God blesses what

He can bless. To reinterpret historical events for any purpose will skew us in our thinking and ultimately in our living. It will take our allegiances and motivation away from God and place them back under self-preservation as if we were never converted.

Let's Consider A Few Questions:

From the viewpoint of eternity, does the religious conservative view of American History really matter in the grand scheme of things?

How is the believer better equipped as a believer by placing value on this country's history?

If this country is indeed important to the Kingdom of God should believers in other countries hold this country's history as dearly as religious conservatives tend to?

Can the history of America teach us anything that we shouldn't already know because we are reading the Bible and listening to God?

What are we saying about our belief if we are unable to deal with what is happening in this world without also fixating on American History or American interests?

What history is truer of the follower of Christ—the one which buttresses a glowing outlook on the country of our birth, or the facts about followers of Christ both in the Bible and throughout church history?

Are we "Americans" because of having been born here? Or have we become the Kingdom of God because we have been spiritually reborn?

These are immense questions that could take volumes to completely exhaust in human debate. The purpose here is not to debate these questions, but just pose them to provoke our thinking. There is too little thinking and too much action before details are comprehensively considered in light of God's Word. We have had the answers to these questions for centuries. The organized church has been guilty of overlooking its source of truth for nearly as long. *Have we learned from history yet?*

Another example of "overlooking" our source of truth and operating in huge error concerns Galileo's predicament with the organized church of his day. He proposed that the earth revolved around the sun and was condemned and placed under house arrest for "heresy" because the hierarchy of the church believed Aristotle's view, that the universe revolved around the earth, for some unknown reason. Never mind the references in the Bible which would indicate that Galileo was correct 2500-years before he, the epitome of science at that time in history, articulated the fact with purely scientific analysis, (*cf.* Job 26:10, Prov. 8:27). Once again the "church" became the perpetrator of great injustice because it was meddling in things based upon ignorance.

The organized church has long ignored its authoritative source of truth. It has done many other injustices on top of the Galileo incident by overlooking what the Living Word of God has to say on a subject. Conservative activists would be quick to point out that "we use some scripture to support our ideas." That is well and fine, but what does all of God's word have to say on the subject of church/state relations? For multiple centuries the institutional church has tried to justify its various extra-curricular activities, e.g. the Inquisitions, the Crusades, burning heretics, selling indulgences [a monetary payment to the church for the eternal forgiveness of sins], military conquest as a means of "conversion," all by using "just a little scripture." It is clear that the organized church has tried to exert control in various areas by moralizing subjects it had no business trifling with! Galileo's case was a prime example. *Have we learned from history yet?*

A New Perspective

The subject of the importance of history and the lack of validity of an *en masse* political push over the past 40-years could be quickly resolved if we went back to scripture as our source of objectivity and truth. The significance, or more correctly the insignificance of recent historical events to the follower of Christ, such as the founding of America, could also be addressed. We could also see that our identity as Christians is not established in the ethnicity or nationality we acquired through entering this world. As followers of Christ we would not be divided against the rest of the Body of Christ around the world by allowing ourselves to maintain an identity with America after conversion, through any telling of history. Finally, we could also see that we would have a better worldview if we didn't cloud it by giving ourselves significance through accepting American History as being anything other than the rise and expected fall of another human empire, even as extraordinary as it has been.

Obtaining a basis for thinking and living through history or theology are both farces! One fellow also had this perspective, at least on history. He wrote: "Alas, I have been *doing* history for nearly forty years and I know how indecisive and how nondefinitive the lessons of history are, and how flimsy is any philosophy or theology which is based on those results. It is sand upon sand."[3] This especially can be noted when these are used to motivate people in directions that cannot be supported by the totality of scripture. These two studies are inventions of the human mind. Objective truth about man, and the only significant history ever told about humanity, can only be found in the Word of God. All else is subjective, manipulative refuse that wastes the mind of any follower of Christ who ponders it.

We do not need to be motivated by anything other than God's written Word and what He shows us to do today. For the believer, history should become just an illustration that merely reinforces what God has already shown us in His Word. If we are being driven by anything, such as history or theology, it is not God but rather the devil or our own sinful desire for control and power that is behind our action. God does not herd people and drive them to militancy. He does not encourage us to provoke others against us by plundering what is theirs. If the religious people do not get their way politically in this country, the cultural environment will escalate into more and more aggressive situations against believers. Historically it always has been this way. *Have we learned from history yet?*

As mentioned before, history gives an added sense of belonging. This goes hand in hand with identity. They are intermingled; one feeds the other. It is unclear which one is more dominant or if they are just mutually dependent. The seeds of mis-identity within the church go back much further in ecclesiastical history than just the American experience. This is another discussion altogether. Yet, it is a fact that mis-identity is another leg of support for the church's affinity with political control. We will entertain this aspect next.

7

Mis-Identity As A Motivator For Political Activism

Dealing with our identity as followers of Christ is a topic that has been written about to near *ad nauseam* in religious circles today. It hardly seems worth mentioning the topic again here, but many church people still struggle with who they really are in Christ and what that means. We will not be diverging into the usual emotional dribble commonly associated with this subject. Rather, I want us to focus more specifically on how we see ourselves in comparison to the secular world around us, and how we need to change the way we live and think based on this comparison.

Concerning political activism, there seems to be a significant connection between who Christian people think they are and what they involve themselves with. In other words, actions expose what we really think of ourselves and who we think we are. It would seem by the evidence available that our identity as believers is not so much based upon what we *say* we believe as Christians, but more eminently where we are with respect to a nationality or a sub-culture as we will see shortly. This reality is quite a problem because of how it divides our minds and therefore our actions. I am referring directly to national identity and how it has been overlaid on our true identity.

Americans do not struggle with coming to terms with being American, it comes rather naturally. Since we are born and educated here, we have no cause to reflect about whether or not we are really American. Compare this to the technical truth from the Bible where we are now disciples, part of another Kingdom when we come to Christ. The former idea of a continued belonging in the world is common to virtually all people in all denominations. This perceived identity is the only common denominator that ties people of differing theological views together in an assemblage such as what conservative political action embodies. This identity is arrived at through a common yet somewhat esoteric view of history which various groupings of believers have ingested. In turn, this has culminated in a common assumption about our identity.

To illustrate the ingrained bias of Christians in this country to identifying ourselves more as being Americans rather than followers of Christ, let's look at some clear evidence. At the end of the WW II General Douglas MacArthur, the commander of the US Army forces in the Pacific, made an impassioned call to America for 10,000 missionaries to help rebuild Japan and evangelize it. This was MacAurthur's real desire over and against the usual practice of having a military occupying force do the work of rebuilding.

Imagine having a high governmental official welcome missionaries to do the work we are supposed to do and should have been doing already. Sadly, only a few hundred missionaries showed up. This single event spoke volumes about how we really thought at that time and that to which we really subscribed. Christians in America blew a perfect opportunity for eternity because they were so propagandized against the Japanese, seeing themselves more as Americans than followers of Christ. Today there is less then seven tenths of a percent Christian population in Japan. This takes into account both liberal and conservative Christian groups together. Unsurprisingly, Japan remains one of the most un-evangelized industrial nations in the world today.

Bob Sjogren, an author, related a story in his book, *Unveiled at Last,* about another recent event in America that reveals we still think the same way about ourselves as we did in the last example.

> Greg Livingstone was scheduled to give a missions minute... *he* stepped up to the podium... *and he* asked, 'How many of you are praying for the 52 American hostages held captive in Iran?' ...All present raised their hands. 'Wow that is terrific there must be 4000 people here. Now let's be honest; because Jesus is watching. How many of you...are praying for the 45 million Iranians held captive in Islam?'... 'What! Only two people? he yelled. What are you guys, Americans first and believers second?' The ensuing silence was not smoothly orchestrated. It was a powerful 60 seconds you will never forget. He closed by saying, 'and I thought I was in a Bible believing church!"[1] *(Italics added for clarity)*

Whew! What a powerful "missions minute." This story forcefully illustrates our thinking that in fact we still see ourselves as Americans, rather than followers of Christ who just happen to live in this country.

Yet there is another more recent example of this same phenomenon from the first Gulf War. On one occasion at an Adult Sunday School class at my church, the class spent significant time in prayer for American soldiers and the war effort. No one seemed concerned for the Iraqi people or their soldiers. Here the Iraqis were being dispatched into an inevitable godless eternity [US Military estimated 85,000 to 120,000 souls killed] and we are praying and cheering for "our boys" who were doing the dirty work?

Have we so identified ourselves as "Americans" that we would side with a political system that is in many ways ungodly, whose activities are less than above board, while still call ourselves followers of Christ?

Are we at the same time identifying with "our boys" who are destroying an unbelieving country, while we are calling ourselves "Christians"?

Have we gone back to the Crusades or what? Does God joy over the Americans winning in battle as one cheers for a football team?

What kind of message are we sending here?

What kind of testimony are we showing to the world at large and non-believers in this country?

Finally, the most recent example of this spectacle of Christians identifying themselves as Americans more than followers of Christ, comes from the response after the terrorist attack on the World Trade Center and Pentagon on September 11, 2001. Once again many Christians revealed that they still identify themselves as Americans primarily, over and against being followers of Christ, because they reacted in the same way as any non-believing person. Many of us responded as victims of a national attack, the same as did those who have no hope in Christ. Nothing could be further from the truth! Instead of being the stable group amidst the worldly-minded around us, we jumped in the same pool as those who are merely temporal-minded, acting as though we were victims too. We should be the ones who are able to reach out to society around us and minister the hope we have, which is in Christ, instead of a hope in a nation's pride or national sovereignty. In blatant disregard of the truth in the Bible about our identity, we lock arms with the secular society around us in consternation, fear and outrage.

How can Christians be so surprised at the evil in the world unless we are in a dream world, out of touch with its reality?

Many Christian leaders went before the news media offering the same whimpering prayers for wisdom and understanding as offered by people of mere religion or even secular people who lack the light of God. Was God surprised at this turn of events on 9-11? There is no evidence to show that ancient Christians lamented when Rome was attacked by the Visigoths or other invaders. They maintained their work and focus, spreading the truth. By the 4th century their influence in the realm became a temptation for the emperor to pilfer. We will expound on this point in later chapters. In making this quick comparison to the past we can see that modern believers have changed in their focus and dependencies and this is not a good change. How far we have fallen!

What we have identified is a major problem for the cause of Christ through the organized church in America. The information we have reviewed in this chapter suggests that Christians are compartmentalizing themselves, living out of many different, independent sub-sections of thought, motivation and identity, rather than a singular identity with, in, and through Jesus Christ. Jesus had an interesting comment concerning duplicity.

No one can serve two masters; for either he will hate the one and love the other, or he will hold to one and despise the other. You cannot serve God and mammon, (*cf.* Matt. 6:24).

This text of course is speaking of money and the danger of it owning us. At the same time there is a principle we can draw from what Christ said: we cannot have two things directing our lives. They will fight against one another.

If our identity is off-base we will be off on tangents in the way we live and conduct our lives. Christians in the West tend to be *Syncretistic-Thinkers*, meaning that we incorporate inconsistencies or irreconcilable ideas into our lives. We compartmentalize things to the point that various aspects of our lives become totally independent and separate from other compartments of thought or identity. The incompatibilities of this mindset are not easily detected nor dealt with by the person who is caught up in it.

Syncretistic-Thinkers are victims of a confused existence. Syncretistic-Thinkers often involve themselves in all sorts of activities that naturally oppose one another in a logical contigutive sense. They can do this without feeling a sense of living a double life. They can live this way because they do not hold any single thing as being primary in their lives. This is *pluralism* and it abounds in the church! We have our self-life, business-life, sex-life, entertainment-life, family-life, our private-life, and public-life; all these appendages to our perceived identity. Pockets of the church have gotten even more compartmentalized in their thinking to encompass more of how they see themselves. Groupings such as: White, African-American, Hispanic, Republican, Democrat, Conservative, Liberal...the list is endless!

One of the key activities of the enemy is to destroy. The quickest way to destroy any group's effectiveness is to divide it. Jesus prayed for unity of the brethren in John 17. The devil has effectively divided people of the church in this country as well as divided our potential effectiveness. Jesus said that a house divided against itself will not stand, (*cf.* Mark 3:25).

The opposite of Syncretistic-Thinkers would be *Integrated-Thinkers.* These individuals see themselves and what they do from one vantage point. Everything they do, or are involved with, emanates from this sole position of identity. There is only one way, and one existence, for the Integrated-Thinker. Everything about the Integrated-Thinker is brought into subjection to one thing: his identity. Everything flows from this initial point. Paul and all of the disciples of Jesus Christ saw themselves one way and everything they did came from this reality. The Apostles could have been involved with any number of things but nothing *owned* them other than the cause of Christ. The Apostles turned the Roman world upside down within several decades after they were exposed to Christ.

Even in the 2nd and 3rd centuries there are many examples of people operating from a single point of identity where all else meant nothing. In a letter from the brethren in Gaul [modern day France] to the Brothers at Phrygia (circa 177AD), the historian Eusebius gives us a glimpse of how the saints of that day saw themselves in comparison to the world. "Sanctus... steadfastly endured tortures beyond all measure...To every question he gave only one answer...I am a Christian instead of giving his name, native city, family...or his race or whether he was slave or free."[2]

Believers operating under false assumed identities have not always been a problem just with believers in America. However, since certain theological ideas have been abandoned around the world in recent decades, followers of Christ outside the United States have mostly given up on the idea of dominating the governments in the countries where they live. So this kind of mis-identity persists mainly as an aberrant behavior of believers in this country.

It is then very important that we reorient our minds to know whom we are related to and just exactly what it means when we become "a new creation" in Christ. We need to become integrated in our living to the fact that, "old things have passed away; behold, *all things have become new,*" (*cf.* II Cor. 5:17 KJV). For years we have glossed over this same verse, which has much more meaning than we have been customarily taught.

Certainly we have the basic understanding that we need to "follow Christ" but it seems like our understanding stops at the ankle-deep level. There does not seem to be the carry-through to a "baptism" into the oceans of truth which encompass our entire lives. It is these deeper understandings which we need to grasp that will dissolve the tendencies we see today of maintaining an identity in the society around us, or expecting the world to coddle us in its bosom. We need to put down into the deep and catch what God is really saying to the church of this present time. We need to loose ourselves from the traditions, involvements and belonging to the state, which the organized church has taught us and begin doing what God wants us to do. Currently, we have been fishing all night (i.e., the past 40-years of political fooling around) and have caught nothing of substance because we are working in our strength and our own way. It is time we cast our lot with the early church and recapture what Christ has been saying to the church's willful deafness for the better part of the last two millennia.

Thus far we have looked at how theology, a self-aggrandizing view of history and mis-identities warp our thinking and send us into left field. Let's take this mis-identity detail a step further and look at the philosophical ramifications. The church's divergence does not stop where it started, lets see where it goes.

8

"We Are Caesar"... Or Are We?

The quote "we are Caesar" was a favorite adage used by various conservative, religious, political groups in the mid-1980's. This phrase was a means in justifying an aggressive participation in the political arena. This axiom intimates that being "Caesar" is part of our identity. Since we have a tendency toward appliqué tutelages that add to what we think of as our identity, we need to identify and unlearn many things which have crept into acceptable teaching in the church in order to do the work God has intended for us.

One accepted ideal that has not been challenged by the modern church is the philosophy of democracy, and it is here that the axiom "We are Caesar" rests. Many might be horrified at a challenge to the validity of followers of Christ zealously cooperating with and propagating the democratic process. We must, however, look beyond the surface of what we currently believe to gain a comprehensive understanding of why we believe it and whether what we believe is true.

It would appear that Christians in America have only considered what they have been taught in school about democracy instead of all that has been said about it, as we shall see. We need to see that other perspectives on democracy exist and that they are worthy of the believer's consideration. We may find that highly venerated ideas are not always right just because we have been taught them. The Western mind, to include that of most Christians, believes that democracy is among the crowning achievements of modern civilization. This simplistic view overlooks the truth that democracy is in fact just one of many culminative products of western civilization just like: Communism, Evolution, and The New-World Order.

These correlations are sad but true. They are sad because so many Christians believe democracy to be positive when in fact it has become just another branch of Humanism,* which they do not seem to understand. The enemy has used democracy as one of the most subtle attacks on the church ever. More so than any other philosophy because democracy's active agent is the believer's own choice to interact for their own benefit. That which is so willing to include us (the church) cannot be bad, can it? Many would find it difficult to identify something as being bad when they profit from its use or employment. This explains why very few Christians have sounded warnings concerning the dangers of democracy.

One of the defining points of democracy is having the ability to use choice in regards to having a specific administration of government over us. More accurately, democracy is the idea of a popular consensus. It can *potentially* be the ability to choose one's government over being forced to make a non-choice, or worse yet to acquiesce in choosing a negative because of the threat of bodily harm. This all seems good to many believers and they would point to various scriptures as a means

---

*Footnote: "Humanism can be defined as the happiness of man is the greatest good" ^therefore all else is subjugated to this end, even morality, laws or any standard..." ^Quoted from Paris Reidhead's sermon, Ten Shekels and a Shirt. Details in Appendix II.

of supporting this positive view, (*cf.* Josh. 24:15b). Being given a choice is considered to be positive, but it is not always. Other than this simple definition of "being able to choose," very few could articulate much else of what democracy is. Let's see what others have said about democracy. A British Professor named Alexander Fraser Tyler once wrote:

Democracy cannot exist as a permanent form of government. It can exist only until voters discover they can vote themselves largess, or a liberal gift, out of the public treasury. From that moment on, the majority always votes for the candidate promising the most benefits from the public treasury, with the result that democracy *always collapses over loose fiscal policy, always to be followed by a dictatorship.*[1]

Tyler's analysis of democracy may come as a slap in the face to those who hold dear this form of government. John Adams also made similar comments when he said, "Remember, democracy never lasts long. It soon wastes, exhausts and murders itself. There never was a democracy yet that did not commit suicide."

Still another perspective comes from an unlikely source; the intellectual, socialist playwright George Bernard Shaw in his 1903 book, *Man & Superman: Maxims for Revolutionists*. Shaw wrote, "Democracy is a form of government that substitutes election by the incompetent many for the appointment by the corrupt few." This statement is a pungent reinforcement of the idea that democracy is dangerous especially when it is in the hands of simple-minded, ignorant people or those who are sly and greedy for power.

For yet another comment on the democratic process of choosing what government offers us we can turn to Pastor Richard Wurmbrand, who spent 14-years in Communist jails, three years in solitary and all under torture. Wurmbrand gave us a warning, "Jesus has told us to discern between the language of seduction and the language of love, and to know the wolves in sheepskin from the real sheep."[2] The language of democracy is indeed the language of seduction for any person, especially the believer. Benjamin Franklin, one of America's most noted early leaders uses a similar word picture to describe democracy. He wrote, "Democracy is two wolves and a lamb voting on what to have for lunch."

Jesus faced the same seductive temptation when He was fasting in the wilderness, (cf. Matt. 4:1-11). Satan tempted Christ with what was rightfully His (Christ's) only that it was to be obtained in an ungodly way. Power and control are as much of a temptation to us today as they were to Christ in that time of temptation. Democracy seduces people into believing they are really in charge and that the government is merely an extension of their beliefs and values. In many ways God is supplanted because people, sadly many believers included, go to the government for answers to problems rather than to God. This is a serious problem!

Another problem is that democracy is not what it is thought to be by many Christians. Many conservatives think that America, which is a representative democracy, is somehow a continuum from its days as a representative constitutional republic in short rule by law. A constitutional republic means that governing is done by law. However, democracy, which is rule by agreement, is a matter of popular opinion.

Democracy is the designation most people in this country use to identify the form of government in America and most Christians would agree to this term. The question then arises, is this country, practically speaking, a democracy or is it a republic? That question is a sticky debate. Some have tried to reconcile the incompatibilities presented by the changes in terminology over the last 60-years by saying that America is a Democratic Republic or a Constitutional Democracy. These terms are simply oxymoronic! There cannot be rule by law and rule by popular vote at the same time. Under the system of democracy, there can only be rule by law through popular vote. But then, law is controlled by what is thought to be popular at the time. Thus law is not a matter of fact, a matter based on absolutes, it becomes whatever seems pleasing to a majority. This majority can change at any moment.

So, if rule is established by popularity under the democratic system, can we really declare and rule by law as the saying, "we are Caesar" would imply? If rule is obtained through popularity then the answer is, not really. Only as long as a majority can be obtained and maintained, can control by anyone or any group be realized. It is clear that democracy is chiefly based on popular vote rather than in law. Since believers are confused into thinking that this country is still under the old constitutional system, it is then necessary to ask some questions and draw some conclusions.

If saying "we are Caesar" means that we as believers have the ability to rule, albeit through voting, then why are the attempts to control the downward spiral of morals and ethics through our alleged "rule" not working in this country?

Either believers in this country are not in the majority, or we must conclude that all the dynamics concerning democracy have not been considered. Many believers go about politics as though we really are "Caesar", a majority that can rule. Yet, none of the conservative platform items have ever been accomplished as they were defined. It must also be admitted that this country is not under the system of constitution and rule by law since courts and popular vote decide what is admissible over what the old constitution would allow. Case in point, judgments concerning separation of church and state, judgments redefining murder to allow abortion, the burying of common law by continuous additions to civil law...and the list goes on.

My point is exactly that we are not "Caesar" because we are not in the majority, and we have not been able to *rule*. This lack of majority is just as Christ said it would be nearly 2000-years ago, (*cf.* Matt. 7:13-14, 9:37). Many conservatives will squabble about this majority detail. But so far, a critical mass of conservatives has not been sustained for any length of time but the steady erosion of morality is not only constant, it's increasing at a precipitous rate. Secondly, the foundations of law and morality have been removed. Therefore, we have nothing to appeal to in society's sense of what is really right, in matters of establishing and maintaining a just mere moral facade, much less a true righteous standing in God's eyes.

I am surprised that we, who believe in a Holy God, waste our time trying to get people to act morally without the gospel, as the basis for being able to be moral, having been addressed in the process. "If the foundations are destroyed, what can the righteous man do?" (cf. Ps. 11:3) If people do not understand the basis for law, if they do not hold to any absolutes, and if they are self-serving rather than God serving, we cannot appeal to them concerning what is right nor why it is right. Since we cannot gain or maintain any majority, we cannot rule. Therefore, the axiom "We are Caesar" for the disciple is baseless and ridiculous!

Of what significance is our belief in what is right if the only means of influence is through a political avenue as the conservatives seem to believe?

A belief in what is right is mere wallpaper if we are trying to mandate mere morality through a political system. We do not have a majority and thus we have lost our means of achieving rightness in society through politics. Church historian Roland Bainton said, "If there is no accommodation [to the culture] Christianity is unintelligible and cannot be spread; if there is too much accommodation it will be spread, but will no longer be Christianity."[2]

It would seem that going exclusively through the political system to change culture is too much of an accommodation. Our talk about morality to this culture means nothing to them and our political efforts thus far have been ineffective by any measure. In effect, the Religious-Right is advocating, *be moral without knowing God.* This is nothing more than a white-washing self improvement program designed by religious people to help us feel more at home in the sinner's ungodly world. Doesn't this sound a bit like Lot in Sodom?

If all we are doing is putting our fingers into all the holes in a dam, holding back total anarchy, we have failed to solve the real problems in the process. In addition, we have preoccupied ourselves with a ruse. We have become fools to think that we can successfully legislate the morality of people through law as an extension of our vote. There is not a big enough voting block to secure the control conservatives desire to put on this country. If all that is left for us to do with our vote is to register our opinion, of what lasting value is that? If politics is sought after from the perspective of "we are Caesar" then we are universes apart in mindset from those who became aliens in their own lands to follow Christ! The only way politics can be a viable means of doing God's work is when God is directing the venture, e.g. Daniel in Babylon, Joseph in Egypt. God's mission in the affairs of men will not become a self-serving means for any group of believers no matter what scripture they use in supporting their view.

...THE MOMENT
ONE SPEAKS OF
"PRESENCE TO THE WORLD"
CHRISTIANS TRANSLATE
THIS AS POLITICAL PRESENCE.
IT WOULD SEEM THAT THERE IS
ABSOLUTELY NO OTHER WAY
TO BE PRESENT
TO THE WORLD OTHER THAN
TO ENGAGE IN POLITICS.

– Jacques Ellul –

9

The Deceptiveness Of Democracy

As was mentioned before, the few facets of democracy most Christians understand are likely the only aspects they might have ever entertained. In the last chapter we looked at a few comments made by notable people that should awaken our interest. What else have we not considered about democracy? The deceptiveness of democracy is that we can supposedly choose the future of this country and control it through voting. The evidence on whether we really can effectively control the moral slide of this country through voting is seriously in question after 40-years of failure. But perhaps a more important question for the believer is, *should we even try*? Some groups call this "taking dominion." Others would say it is being a good steward of the opportunity God has given us. Many of these would point to a few texts of scripture, mostly in the OT, to prove their point of seeking to affect culture through the means of politics.

Consider for a moment what today's medicine is able to do that was only be dreamed about for centuries. Most recently, with the unlocking of the genetic code, the implications of what can be done through the science of medicine are vastly extended. With this coming of age in modern medicine, many questions concerning morals and ethics have come back into the forefront. People want to know what is ethical or even moral. Given the new horizons science offers mankind, how do we decide what is right or wrong, ethical or moral? This problem, what new discoveries do to old paradigms of morality, is a microcosm of what has become an icon of modern society that includes the church. Things have slipped from what was clearly right or wrong, to becoming mere shades of gray. Who is to say what is really right? Is there really a thing called "right" in an absolute sense?

Have technology and discovery changed morality or caused a need to redefine what we once thought to be moral?

There is a question that is more preeminent than the question, *"is it right or wrong."*

Just because we have the ability to do something, does this mean we should do it?

The answer to this question is even more important than the other questions or their answers. The answer is, *not always!*

Why is it so important to consider if a choice should be made or not? Among other things, the *"relegation of chooser"* is of utmost importance, especially for the believer. Relegation means where do our choices automatically put us as far as outcome, ramification or identification. What do our choices relegate us to be?

Is every available choice one in which we should participate, just because it is being put in front of us?

If you said "no," we are going in the right

direction. Eve should have considered her choices in the garden more carefully. Where did her choice to eat the fruit relegate her and her posterity?

What does "relegation of the chooser" have to do with the deceptiveness of democracy?

Sometimes we can choose things that automatically put us into an arena we should not be caught dead in as representatives of Christ. If the world can put the follower of Christ into a straitjacket mentally or philosophically, it will limit our effectiveness. The enemy knows this and has been behind the scenes fomenting all kinds of traps for Christians to fall into and we have been falling into them for centuries. The enemy loves for us to walk off the narrow path of Christ's calling for our lives in order to dilly-dally in the world's *Vanity Fair*.[1]

The strangeness of our day is that the societal system of politics through the means of democracy has offered two regimens of destruction to the church and we have not grasped the reality of this paradox. Those who loosely bandy scripture about claiming to be following it are simplemindedly falling into a trap in which most any choice, save the one God *may* show us to make, is a losing proposition.

To illustrate, let's consider making a choice between two negative things like an overdose of either methamphetamine or heroin. This might seem to be an absurd analogy, which is the point. It illustrates what is happening in this country politically. No matter who is running things over the past 70-years, be it Republican or Democrat, there has been a steady downward trend morally, ethically, spiritually and in most other respects save the economy. Rush Limbaugh has repeatedly depicted this reality on his radio show when he compared the political rhetoric of John F. Kennedy in the early 1960's to the Republican language of today. In other words, today's Republicans have stooped to the level of the Democrats of the 1960's while many of today's Democrats have plunged into ideals and approaches that are pure degradation and deceit.

The nature of politics/democracy is issue-based. Issues have become the great equalizers and power-brokers. Richard John Neuhaus once wrote, "It is in the interest of politicians and the hordes of people who make their living by talking about what politicians do to *disguise the stark and simple truth that they are engaged in the getting and keeping power.*"[2] Issues are a means of getting power. Issues are also a natural means of dividing people into groups. Once people put themselves into these politically defined groups they become easy to manipulate. Purposed division like this should sound an alarm with all believers because it is the first step towards destruction. A house divided against itself will not stand, (*cf.* Mark 3:25). "The *house* of God," or at least those who charade about being the "house of God," is certainly *divided* over politics!

What does this obvious division tell us about the political parties and their objectives and purposes?

Many folks, including the religious, believe that political parties are headed towards the objective of an issue that a group of constituents are following. The politically active do not conceive that, for the politician or his party, any issue is merely a means to an end rather than an end in and of itself. The "end" is power; not justice, equity, voice or even change for which most issues were cultivated. This is the absurdity of political action. Nothing is ever finished, it is always just in process. Another absurdity is that if the government ever attempts to fix something it is more screwed up afterwards and so the process continues to right the situation, e.g., Medicaid, Social Security and drug cards.

The vast majority of recent political history can be recounted as evidence of this analysis. As for more specific evidence of a political party's shallow relationship to the essence behind an issue of a special interest group, consider that in the years from 1996 till 2002 the Republican Party was ready to "dump" the religious conservative "platform issues." A faction in the Party thought conservatism was more of a liability than an asset to winning high offices. This is a prime indication that parties merely use special interest groups and their issues to gain power.

Let us look at another illustrative scenario that will paint a picture of the problems we face when we try to stop this country's moral slide through political means. On one hand, you have a candidate who is great on foreign policy and social reform but is also soft on abortion and liberal about the homosexual agenda. Conversely, the opposing candidate has a tough stand on abortion and is against the homosexual agenda, while he is completely clueless regarding social reform and foreign policy. What should we do as believers? Is this really a choice or is it moral or nationalistic suicide? Those who vote exclusively according to "morally based issues" will find themselves voting for the lesser of two evils and usually the less capable of the two politically. I would challenge anyone to find scriptural support for this "lesser of two evils" approach! Don't even mention voting Independent. It's a waste, if the real goal is to effect change, the independent has no chance of winning.

On top of what the politicians are trying to do, the proponents of political activism are playing theological games based on false assumptions of identity, history and weird interpretations of scripture when they advocate involvement in the political realm using the motivations and explanations they give. On the one hand, the activist tells us that we are supposed to be patriots as well as Christians, which is pluralism, (*cf.* Matt. 6:24, Jas. 1:5-8 4:8). On the other hand, the political system gives us the choice of being either a patriot or a follower of Christ, through various choices, should we choose to make them. Both of these options have destructive outcomes. It is not a win/win situation. It's very much a win/lose situation. If we should win from one way we really lose from the alternative. If we really are believers and we make any kind of choice under these circumstances, we are fools!

With the political system being the way it is, constituents are forced to swallow the good with the bad. With religious thought the way it is today believers are made to think that their only avenue to effect change is through the political system. On top of this they proceed in this venture without a concerted effort in prayer and seeking God about what should be done. Supposedly, scripture has given us all that we need, but off we go into the political wild blue yonder based solely on our limited views and interpretations, with a very suspicious use of scripture, I might add. On the other hand, if we ask God what to do based upon a full knowledge of the scriptures, His directives may not include the agenda the activists advocate.

Could we be seeing scripture incorrectly or could we be looking at issues wrongly and responding in a way that God would not want?

No one will ever know without asking God, and this does not seem to be the *modus operandi* of political activism. King David inquired of the LORD, saying, "Shall I go up against the Philistines? Wilt Thou give them into my hand?" And the LORD said to David, "Go up, for I will certainly give the Philistines into your hand," (*cf.* II Sam. 5:19). And at other times God said to Israel, "Do not go up, lest you be struck down before your enemies, for the LORD is not among you," (*cf.*

Num. 14:42). There does not seem to be a balanced view widely available to believers today from religious leaders. Either we are told to be immersed in political activism or we are told to abstain from the "dirty work of the world."

Where is the teaching that encourages the believer to listen to God and seek what He wants rather than what seems the right thing to do based on our point of view?

Many of today's believers do not even possess a rudimentary understanding of church history. In the early church, leaders were faced with similar options to what democracy presents us today. For 300-years the church had been tortured, chased, harassed, dogged, made death sport of, pillaged and many other nasty things. In time the state offered the church reprieve through edict, recognition so as to become part of the state. Few events in history have changed the church more for the negative than this specific incident.

In the words of one author, "In fact, there may have been no greater disaster for the cause of the gospel, in contrast to the material interests of the clerical class, than the marriage of the church and state which first occurred under Constantine...*this* adulterous affair destroyed the church's independence and position of moral leadership."[3] Of course this proposal by the State sounded good to the beleaguered church of that time. What could be wrong with not being an outlaw anymore? Yet as we look back, the church was forever changed by this single choice, and this change was not good. The church became an institution rather than a fellowship of Christ's suffering.

We might think, "Well, I am glad I live in these days where I can be *'free'* to practice my belief." Yet it is this very thing, state sponsored freedom, that fetters the church. We now waste our life and limb defending our "freedoms" provided by the state instead of expending our lives doing what God asked us to do. And besides, how much "freer" can one be than the one whom the Son sets free? The original church had no "freedom" granted by the state and it did not matter because they lived as citizens of Heaven, (cf. Phil. 3:20).

The early church concentrated their efforts on being whom they really were rather than trying to maintain what the state had afforded them. Jesus said "For whoever wishes to save his life shall lose it; but whoever loses his life for My sake and the gospel's shall save it," (cf. Mark 8:35). This is true in all aspects of life. If we in our own strength for our own purposes try and maintain what we think is ours we will lose it. Through political activism we may even lose a lot more than state sponsored freedom.

The deceptiveness of democracy is that we step out of our element when we step en masse onto the political stage set up by the enemy. The opportunity afforded by the democratic system is more of a temptation like the lottery than any real opportunity. The stakes for which we are tempted to play politics obscure the cost to the believer/church for having played. These same stakes for which we play the game of politics are no more secured for having played either. The distraction of democracy dilutes the church in purpose, identity and effectiveness. Democracy is like a black hole, which sucks everything into its grip and utterly cuts off any counteractive work or ability to respond to anything but its demands. The question is, when is "the church" going to wake up and smell the coffee? And when they do, what will they do about it?

10

Other Concerns About Politics

There are several other questions that are not adequately addressed by conservative political activists. While the activists articulate many reasons for their approach and the need for it, they do not address the fact that what they advocate flies in the face of other "beliefs" they claim to hold. When you take into account that these inconsistencies deal with major themes in Christian teaching our interest should really be piqued. If God was in this charade of corporately using politics as the chief means for the church to do its job (as many proponents would like you to think it is), don't you think the negative features we covered in Chapter 3, *Stupid Is As Stupid Does*, could not be associated to the church's people who have joined in this activity?

Who can point to any "failure" in the Bible (like that of modern conservative Christians in their political activities) being the direct result of doing what God told someone to do, wherein they were following His exact directions?

Divisiveness In The Ranks Of The Church

A notable concern is what politics is doing to the church as far as divisiveness. Former Senator Mark O. Hatfield once said,

> Let me take off my political hat and put on my layman's hat. I'm more concerned as to what political activism is doing to the gospel. When you label something "Christian," if it is accompanied by an agenda of political items and the economic items on that agenda of political action, does that mean that if you agree with the political items and the economic items on the agenda that that constitutes your Christianity? No way! Christ asked Peter one question. It was not "who do others say that I am," but "who do you say that I am?" That is the basic question. People outside the faith get the wrong message. They think, "Well, if I believe in these political issues because they say this is the 'Christian' agenda, then I'm a Christian." And that is to me miscommunication. That is not biblical. The question is, who do you say Christ is? – Not who agrees about abortion or school prayer.[1]

Dean Sherman, an international speaker and author with Youth With a Mission, shows his concern with the churches deviated activities. He wrote,

> Even Christians can take action in the wrong way. Many well-meaning folks give money, time, and efforts to improving man's situation, but ignore the spiritual way to combat evil. They are more concerned with man's condition than with God's heart. They attend protests, organize boy-

cotts, or launch educational efforts, but spend little or no time in prayer, spiritual warfare, or evangelism.[2]

Additionally concerning divisiveness, it is odd when people who claim to have the same belief and who also claim dependency on God for decisions of importance come up on opposite sides of the same issue. In the same race there are "Christians" supporting both sides. In other words, one votes Democrat and the other Republican. Why? If we really are following the *same God*, either we have to change our definition of the *same God* or we have to throw out that we are really *following* that same God.

Does God have "Multiple Personality Disorder"?

Is God telling one person one thing and another person the opposite? Surely not! (*cf.* I Cor. 1:10-13)

The only other possible explanation for this opposing phenomenon seems to be that people are making up their minds on politically presented issues while only passively assenting to following Christ. If this is true, it says three things about these voters.

1. Their identity is compartmentalized, pluralistic; thus their actions are inconsistent with their claimed beliefs.

2. They are not living out of God's daily word to them; i.e., Jesus' example of doing just what He heard His Father saying... (*cf.* John 5:30, 6:38, 8:28)

3. They are duped into being pawns in the political manipulation game, allowing themselves to be the bow by which the political fiddle is played.

Are believers merely throwing God's name behind what they do to try to legitimize their actions?

Prophets in the OT paid a high price for putting God's name on what they were saying. If we want to vote because we'll feel better, go right ahead! Just don't moralize it or try to pull "God" in on your side by throwing His name behind what you do by saying, *"I'm led of God."*

While we're at it, we shouldn't refer to our "Christian beliefs" as a basis for our choices because they're not. Our identity as an American is our chief motive. Our "Christian beliefs" are just a perspective at best and wall decorations at worst. Instead of listening to God and operating out of what He is showing us, we make ourselves part of the divisiveness of politics rather than being *salt and light* to the society that is being politically manipulated through the issues politicians drum up. We are to be a counter-culture, not one side or the other of the world's game.

The Question Of God's Sovereignty

The Sovereignty of God is also touched in this mess of politics in the church. The proponents of activism really put themselves into a corner on this point because they put such a high emphasis on man's intervention while God's sovereignty is not addressed. The silence of activists on this point gives some indication of what they really believe. It also shows us a major weakness in their position. When we speak of sovereignty we mean control over or complete knowledge of everything. In other words, God allows things if He does not actively direct them.

If we really believe God to be sovereign we should take our hands out of the political stew *until God directs us*, thereby allowing God to do what He wants. We cannot make broad-brushing statements that God wants us to vote, because this cannot be proven. If we say that God wants us to vote without question, then we must face the problem of why believers end up voting against each other, which cannot be God's intent. If God were really telling us to vote, there would be a more decisive direction from religious political action in societal life because of that voting. That however is not the case. If voting were nothing more than the apparatus of man, outcomes would be hit and miss, just like they are. God is still bigger than this, but why cloud our minds as to the sovereignty issue through our meddling?

God's work is simple and decisive, not haphazard. What does scripture tell us? "The king's heart is like channels of water in the hand of the LORD; He turns it wherever He wishes," (*cf.* Prov. 21:1). The only problem today is that we have supposedly been "empowered" by the state and this somehow fogs our minds into thinking God's will cannot be accomplished without our intervention. Maybe the OT scriptures aren't for today simply because we have the vote and a democratic system. Does this "new" option supersede or preclude scripture? This is very shaky ground when we interpret scripture through the perspective of our situations.

It is easy to nod in full agreement with the Bible's record of God's dealings with people and situations, despite kings or rulers. It seems to be quite another story to practically apply allowing God and depending on Him to work things out. Most of us evangelical, fundamental types believe with all our hearts that God is sovereign. However, we are the ones screaming the loudest about cultural reform through the political process. This is not trusting God. The activist mindset places itself as a strategic operative ready to manhandle something that we are not equipped to overcome using the method of politics.

Nationalism

From a scriptural perspective, since when is nationalism a motive for a believer to be propelled into political action?

There is a phrase in the NT repeated in various forms 11 times* that says, "There is no distinction between Greek or Jew." The significance of this phrase is that the Jewish disciples really struggled with this problem of national pride and race superiority because of their "chosen-ness" as Jews, (*cf.* Acts 9:32-10:35). Jesus made a veiled reference that He had followers in "another fold," and that they and the Jewish believers would become one flock with Him, (*cf.* John 10:16). These texts should expose the weakness of nationalism and abolish this idea for the Body of Christ around the world. Especially the kind which seeks to put God on one country's side or against another. Regarding all these scriptures one writer said this: "Few things are said as plainly in the NT, and as often, as that Christ's church is not coextensive with any socio-political grouping or ethnic delineation, and that boundaries are meaningless in it." [3]

God is looking to find people who are willing to voluntarily come out of the world, serve Him and live out of the destiny of their relationship with Him, rather

*Footnote:** These texts speak of a renewal in which God accepts all kinds of people through faith. The Jewish disciples had been pretty exclusive with the truth up until the time of Peter and Cornelius in Acts 9-10. Paul articulates clearly that God does not favor one nation over others. For the 10 scriptures I mentioned above see: Acts 15:9, Rom. 1:14-16, 2:9-26, 3:22, 10:12, I Cor. 1:24, 12:12-13, Gal. 3:28, Eph. 2:11-22 and Col. 3:5-11.

than eating the scraps of garbage that fall off the world's table. Those who advocate political activism do not seem to have made this jump. Nationalism is a system of thought that would tie us back into the world's mindset and keep us sitting below its table waiting for our portion. If we are using the world's system to legitimize or protect us, we need to repent!

God is not an American and He has no eternal interest in this country. He is interested in each person and his or her soul's condition. God is not cheering when America beats the Chinese on trade deficits, or who broke the sound-barrier first. He could not care less! Dr. Tony Evans, founder of the Urban Alternative in Dallas, Texas, had this to say: "Jesus is not an American, He is not a Republican or Democrat. He didn't come to take sides, He came to take over."

Some would say this is a statement from dominion theology. On the contrary! Dr. Evans is saying that God has a separate show going on; it is called the church, the Kingdom of God. It was meant to overrun the world's system, not get in the mud and play with it. Keith Green elaborates on Dr. Evans comments saying, "The original church was the welfare board, soup kitchen, the pregnancy counseling clinics and employment agency, they were all these things and more. Now look at us, oh sure, we still are God's representation on the earth. But can people see it, and if they can't how will they?"[4]

The Forbidden Zone

Recently, I watched the original *Planet of the Apes* movie. This film was quite lucid in its depiction of people [in this case apes] who cannot, or will not, think beyond limits that they have arbitrarily established for themselves. I am not advocating wanton willy-nilly forays into the obscurity of questioning just to question. Rather, I am saying that we need to go beyond what is commonly thought today because most indicators would show that we have been living and thinking on the "safe" side of the forbidden zone.

In the movie, the safe side of the forbidden zone was the intentional denial of reality for a self-serving purpose. The leading "religious" apes in the story denied the evidence in the "forbidden zone" because it did not support their interpretation of events which in turn supported their power and prejudices. In like manner the modern conservative also lives in a theological "safe-zone" which empowers their way of dealing with the alter-reality they've invented. And because we act upon *imaginary reality,** in a very real world, we have become utterly ineffective in our attempts politically as well as in doing what God has commanded us in the Great Commission. Look at Chapter 2, *The State Of Things In The Church In America,* for statistical data.

You might wonder how much involvement or disassociation I am advocating here. I want to de-emphasize the two extremes of being either totally "for" or "against" political involvement. I would rather underline our responsibility as followers of Christ, who are citizens of Heaven, not of the kingdoms of men. This will mean letting go of the imagined ability to control society through voting. However, this does not totally exclude voting or even running for office. More importantly I want to emphasize listening to God and doing exactly, no more or less than, what He tells us.

*Footnote: "Imaginary reality" We are not what we were before we came to Christ. This deals with ethnicity, nationality, denominationalism, and our political identities. To approach the world as if we are still "of it" is a reversal of the truth, i.e. an imaginary reality. This imaginary reality is carried out further in the idea that we can appeal to people to be moral without knowing the gospel basis for morality. When we approach politics with these erroneous ideas we are living in a world that does not really exist.

If that means not responding to the issues the political system pitches over our plate, so be it. For the vast majority of us, we'll not have much to do with the political system because of its intrinsic nature and because of our weaknesses as disciples to understand and participate in the dirt in which politics tends to be played. Few have actually been called to the vocation of politics by God. This is evidenced through failures, burnout and the sudden metamorphosis of "good candidates" that suddenly become functionaries of the system they were elected to fight against.

While modern thinkers advocate the corporate domination of the political system in this country by church people, we need to realize that this is just a modern idea. Let's be reminded that God only used a small group of people who were at the top of their fields, or who were pliable in His hand, to work directly in the political systems of their day. They were exceedingly successful by any measure. God Himself put Daniel, Moses, David, Joseph, Jonathan, Samuel and the Judges into political positions to do His bidding. God's purposes were accomplished in His work through these people and He did not need democracy to do it. This goes back to the issue of God's sovereignty!

The political system of our day allures people with the opportunity of "free choice" and the "potential" to affect things for our own purposes, only not really. It is a trap and a distraction to follow after something other than God. God says come and die and I will raise you up to do the work I have for you. Conservatives condemn gambling and the lottery but with glorious inconsistency they will commonly play a political "lottery" without conscience. Certain people in ministry today think that we should turn lights on in Washington and force the issues. The Bible says "turn The

Light" on in people's heart and things will automatically change because God is calling the shots. Which will you do? Are you going to continue to sin the sin of futility and frustrate the work of God that could be realized through your life because you are off on your own crusade or on somebody else's agenda you have adopted?

Count Zinzendorf, founder of the Moravian Brethren, once said, "I could not spend my time over such trifles as make up the daily life of courtiers and of Kings. I dare not appear before God with the responsibilities incurred by frittering away my days in such puerilities."[5] It should be noted that Zinzendorf did not make this comment out of ignorance regarding the political process. He stepped back from court life after many years in it and took up the work of the Kingdom of God exclusively. He never wanted to participate in the political arena but was "forced" to by certain pressures of his day to do so. Eventually he made a break from this "pressure" and the world has never been the same since.

It is this kind of true commitment to the cause of Christ that needs to resurface in the church today. 10,000-years from now the position we took on most politically manufactured issues will not matter. However, if we do not tell people about the Savior and their inability to achieve what God would give them through this Savior, THAT will make a tremendous difference 10,000-years from now! We need to become fishers of men, not the proponents of political interest groups trying to get the government to see things our way, while we become their lackey in the process, instead of God's servants.

11

So What

Where is all of this taking us? We have outlined theology that could motivate a person in the wrong direction. We have looked at history that gives significance where none is needed. We have looked at ideas that help make people operate under false assumptions of identity. But what does all this mean? Let's treat the situation of the church's deviation into *en masse* politics as if it is a new crime scene.

A detective looks for motives or causation factors in an investigation. While no one can speak for people's thoughts indicting them of improper motives certainly a case can be made for being lured away by someone else's motives, or being "caught up in the spirit of a thing." It is very apparent that the proponents of conservative political activism are very committed to their cause, so motive is very important to this discussion. Proverbs 16:2 tells us that, "All the ways of a man [*or a group*] are clean in his own sight, but the Lord weighs the motives." This text suggests that God is watching, not for what is done necessarily but more importantly, what is behind what is done, i.e., motives.

The actions of men and details concerning their activity suggest motive. Maybe a person means well in his endeavors to "get involved." One could be swept up into "action" with the best of intentions. This does not diminish the spirit/motive of what one has joined. I believe this describes many believers who "act" in the political realm under the dubious guise of engaging society in a "culture war." This actual war took place many years ago and the forces of conservative activism are merely trying to hold on to the last traces of that which has already gone over the cliff. At the same time, conservatives do not understand all the dynamics and ramifications wrapped up in that with which they involve themselves.

Some who joined the Hitler Youth and other auxiliary Nazi programs did so out of a sense of duty to their country. That seems good, right? Did the good intentions of these individuals take away from the real motives or the ramifications of the movement they joined? Not hardly! This analogy illustrates that people can get caught up with involvements that are not what they seemed to be. If people in Germany could have known how the war would end for the Nazis, 98% of the willing but ignorant people would not have joined.

At this point I should emphasize that the people who are into conservative activism are not the same as Nazi sympathizers in comparison to what they are doing and the motives behind it all. Conservatives are similar to those who went along with Nazi programs from the viewpoint that they are involved with something that is not what it seems to be.

Can anyone declare for a fact that political activism, on the scale we see today in the church, is not a trap or distraction from the enemy?

If we cannot see that this is possible, we are already on our way to being deceived, if we are not there already. Who can say that they know for a fact that God is instructing them to do what they are doing as activists, while being able to point to the entirety of what scripture as a basis of support? This would be in comparison to those who take only a few texts for support while downplaying or avoiding the rest, as well as not even giving God a chance to direct their actions.

What can anyone point to in the person and work of Jesus Christ as a precedent for their actions in political activism?

Many would say this question is unfair because Jesus' time on earth was short and He had other things to do. That assertion might hold water. But can precedent be found in the work of the Apostles? If we say that neither Christ nor the Apostles had the opportunity to be involved with the government over them, thus negating any opportunity "to be Caesar," we nullify any way of finding support or disproval for our ideas of *political activism* by the only authoritative source we have, i.e. the Word of God. If we should take the current mind set of the religious conservative activist, inadvertently we invalidate scriptures' applicability to our situation. This is very dangerous ground! These questions and analysis leave the "Christian" activists in jeopardy of either being very ignorant or hypocritical. In addition, the activist certainly cannot be following the person they claim to be following, if they cannot find Him doing what they are doing.

As I mentioned earlier, the common ground of false identities tie many believers of differing theological groups together under one cause. Orthodox Calvinists and Arminians march practically in lock step with "Dominionists" who are also joined by a plethora of other groups including Charismatics. *Why?* The answer certainly is not theological unity. The answer begins with the fact that they see themselves as Americans rather than just followers of Christ. Therefore, since they are still Americans in their mind's eye, what is happening to America, as far as the moral freefall, is then a threat to their personal security. Stanley Hauer-was wrote, "Martin Luther called security the ultimate idol. And we have shown, time and time again, our willingness to exchange anything; family, health, church, and truth for a taste of security."[1]

Religious conservatives know correctly that God will eventually judge this country, as He has judged every other culture that has divested itself of Him and His law. The problem is that since activists see themselves as Americans rather than their true identity as followers of Christ, they have gone after and contended for their own selfish agenda. Deeper than theological motivations, deeper than mis-identities that lead to improper associations, deeper than motives based on a legacy derived from an illegitimate history, is the root of selfishness.

Many in church today have become manipulators for their own purpose, security as a part of society rather than being the ministers that God has called them to be. We are all called to be ministers who bring God into people's lives through being *salt and light,* rather than loudmouths for our own gain and security in the public square. True ministers do not try and force their morality, much less any selfish motivations, on the seculatists around them. True ministers do their work for love of God and His love of people. Anybody who walks with "Dominionists" in their weakness does not understand that God is not so concerned that people obey and live by His law as much as He wants them to be motivated by the love of Christ and knowing Him. This will go beyond keeping the law. The only way this will happen is if people's hearts are *transformed*!

Transformation will not happen in the halls of power in this country or any other. Obeying biblical law failed to perfect man to God's standard under the first covenant. That is why there was need for a second one. Transformation is then paramount to affecting change;

it is the carrier of change! Change is not the goal; it is an outflow of the goal. Salvation, people coming into a right relationship with God, is the beginning of the right direction. The goal is loving God. This will have an absolutely profound effect on people's lives and work. Transformation will only happen in the hearts of men as believers realize their role is to become disciples and obey God's command to convey the truth of His love to all they meet.

God does not require anyone to keep the law regardless of a relationship with Him. "It is true that God will reward a nation/*person* that follows Him *(i.e., His Law)*, Ps. 33:12, but God requires heartfelt obedience, not formalistic obeisance."[2] Sure there will be certain consequences that naturally follow disobedience, but everybody has a choice. The unregenerate cannot obey God's Law nor will they want to because of their wicked hearts. While unbelievers may externally obey God for one reason or another, their hearts remain black, disobedient and rebellious as ever. Zinzendorf, who met earlier, once said, "It is impossible to put the yoke of Christ on men against their will and until they have been converted. To exercise an external constraint, to forbid worldly diversions, is the way to make hypocrites, and to produce the most frightful secret abomination. It also is the way to make men satisfied with themselves, simply because they abstain from those diversions with which others sometimes amuse themselves."[3] Sinners will keep God's laws and live as examples to all if they come to know Him first. They will otherwise obey only if there is something in it for them, or as long as there is an exterior pressure keeping them in line.

Do the people who promote Dominionism through political activism want people to obey out of impure motives or a mindless exterior compliance?

The identity Christians in this country have maintained—of being American—binds them together in an assemblage that is opposed to what the profession of Christ as Lord means. Today's rendition of "conversion" has failed to break down these false identities that believers continue to assume. To top it off, theology often acts as a catalyst, an intensifier, to send people off the deep-end in activities which have nothing to do with who or what they really are as followers of Christ. Biblically reforming society is not our directive! However, the transformation of people anywhere and everywhere by what we have come to know in Christ is what we have been commanded to do throughout scripture. Society will follow the people because the society is composed of people. If you deal with people's hearts, their hearts will deal with their actions. One fellow wrote:

> The Lord works from the inside out. The world works from the outside in. The world would take people out of the slums. Christ takes the slums out of the people and then they take themselves out of the slums. The world would mold men by changing their environment. Christ changes men, who then change their environment. The world would shape human behavior, but Christ can change human nature.[4]

The church needs to be revived because it is diluted in teaching, focus, and mission. We have left the ballpark of influencing people for eternity and have gone into another arena of manipulating society for our temporal and self-serving purposes. Jesus did not say to go into the entire world and take dominion in every area of life and subject everyone to God's biblical moral law so that the world's cultures will be reformed and you will be more comfortable while living there. He did, however command, "Go therefore and make disciples of all nations, baptizing them in the Name of the Father and the Son and the Holy Spirit, teaching them to observe all that I commanded you."

The Moravians were a group of believers who were sold out to evangelism and life-change in and through the work of Christ and the Holy Spirit. During the late 1700's and into the early 1800's they were said to account for nearly 50% of all missionaries world-wide. They breathed spiritual destiny into men like John and Charles Wesley and thus early Methodism and the Wesleyan movement.

One story about the Moravians stirs me greatly. Two of their group heard of an island in the Caribbean where all religious influences was forbidden. So moved by this circumstance and by the lack of testimony for Christ in that place, the two sold themselves into slavery so as to be admitted to that island and to pay for their one-way trip. They were never heard from again! This account makes the modern attempt of using political activism to do the churches' job, seem cheap, stupid and frivolous by comparison! As they set sail these two men were heard to say, "May the Lamb that was slain receive the reward for which He is worthy."[5] We would do well to consider whether God is receiving that which He is worthy of through our "culture wars" and through our political fooling around!

WHAT INFLUENCE IN FACT
HAVE CHRISTIAN
ECCLESIASTICAL ESTABLISHMENTS
HAD ON CIVIL SOCIETY?
IN MANY INSTANCES THEY
HAVE BEEN UPHOLDING THE
"THRONES OF POLITICAL TYRANNY"
...RULERS WHO WISHED TO SUBVERT
THE PUBLIC LIBERTY HAVE FOUND
IN THE CLERGY
CONVENIENT AUXILIARIES.

– James Madison –

Section 2

The Classroom of Remedial Learning

TODAY, IT IS FAR MORE
IMPORTANT THAT THE
CHURCH RECOVER HER SENSE
OF IDENTITY AS THE BODY OF
CHRIST...THAN THAT SHE
SHOULD ISSUE STATEMENTS
WITHOUT WEIGHT OR
SIGNIFICANCE, STATEMENTS
WHICH ARE IN NO SENSE A
PRESENCE OF THE KINGDOM,
BUT WHICH, MORE OFTEN
THAN NOT, ARE A WAY OF
EASING THE COLLECTIVE
CONSCIENCE ABOUT EVENTS
FOR WHICH ONE FEELS
RESPONSIBLE WITHOUT BEING
ABLE TO DO ANYTHING
ABOUT THEM.

– Jacques Ellul –

12

Where Do We Go From Here?

Most people in this country, regardless of their background, tend to be accomplishment oriented. In addition to the attitude of "get things done," triumphing in an achievement is even more important. This drive was epitomized by the late football great Vince Lombardi when he said, "Winning isn't everything, it's the only thing." I am not advocating this attitude but merely using it as an illustration of the tremendous value placed on success in America.

This same motivation drives the push for reforming this country through an attempt at church based domination of policy and culture. The problem with the objective behind this phenomenon is that it is misguided. It detracts us from the real objective. Speaking about the accomplishments of the religious conservative movement, one author had this to say, "the political reform movement has *not produced social reformation.* The short history of the *Christian Right* to date can be expressed in three phrases: elation with electoral victories; disappointment when these victories produced no fruit; and, finally, discouragement when important elections were lost."[1]

So if this approach is incorrect, as recent historical evidence indicates, then what should we do?

It is not enough to critique any approach in brutal facts. If justified this is a good place to start. Luther critiqued the religious approach of his day by nailing 95 theses on the Chapel door in Wittenberg, Germany. In our own day we must be willing to address the problems head-on and then find a positive direction from the critical analysis of what is happening in the religious political activities of the church.

Some may feel that we have spent our time thus far tearing down what others have methodically built up. Initially, Luther's 95 theses were seen this way. But look at outflow of Luther's critique long-term. Many would now look back at Luther with a positive notion. I am hoping that in our day the initial shock over this work will be displaced by a greater understanding of who we are and that our involvements would be more effective for the Kingdom.

This book is an effort to redirect momentum, not to condemn. There are strongholds within the church populace that need to be addressed and broken down. This does not happen by denial or soft pedaling a matter. We as the church are the benefactors of somebody else having gone to bat against the accepted, but wrong, thinking of their day. Why would we think there are not significant problems in our day that need to be challenged in the same way? Challenges are not a picnic but they render good changes.

If reform is what the Religious-Right wants, why are they are so resistant to it themselves?

Is it because they think they are right and every-body else is wrong?

Resistance to change, the attitude that everybody else is out of sorts, is the point where we need to begin our work. Spiritual warfare has to do with breaking down wrong ideas, prejudices, and the drive behind willfully wrong behaviors, or even wrong behaviors that have gained a wide acceptance. We generally direct our mindset on spiritual warfare towards problems in the pagan world. Yet, spiritual warfare is not something that we should always be directing outside the camp of the Lord. We, as humans, though forgiven and justi-fied, can be affected or under the effects of strongholds as sure as anyone else.

In the details surrounding the political affinities of the church, there is much in the way of spiritual warfare that needs to be done. There are age-old philosophies that have crept into the church and have become so entrenched that they are seen as the gospel. These need to be broken down. Many that are sympa-thetic to the ideas of activism are not willing to think about "other" ideas or of taking a different approach. This type of stubbornness is an additional stronghold residing within the church that needs breaking.

Those who came before us were not perfect, just as we are not perfect. Any wrongness associated with efforts to reform the church in the past were not bad per se. There is always fallibility in the efforts of people. The incorrectness associated with these efforts should be the point from which we should begin to repair and go beyond. Church history is like a relay race. One runner hands his baton to the next runner and so on until *the end* when Christ judges the earth.

If there is failure or shortcoming on the part of those before us, we should not continue in their way. Nor should we berate them for their incorrectness. Instead we should identify the wrong and plot a more precise course to go beyond our predecessors and become more effective by drawing closer to God. The correct use of history lies in gaining perspective on what has happened and what things to avoid. God will direct us in applying what His Word says to our lives and work so that we are meeting His purposes. Paul spoke of building carefully on the foundation that has already been laid, (*cf.* I Cor. 3:9-13).

"For we are God's fellow workers; you are God's field, God's building. According to the grace of God, which was given to me, as a wise master builder, I laid a foundation, and another is building upon it. *But let each man be careful how he builds upon it. For no man can lay a foundation other than the one which is laid, which is Jesus Christ. Now if any man builds upon the foundation with gold, silver, precious stones, wood, hay, straw, each man's work will become evident; for the day will show it, because it is to be revealed with fire; and the fire itself will test the quality of each man's work.*

The "building upon" that has gone on in recent years, namely the push into political activism by conservative religious people, is not quality, but merely building on the traditions of men—wood, hay and stubble. Christ sternly rebuked the Pharisees for trading off the commands of God for their own traditions.

How can we not see the correlation between the Pharisees' abandonment of the commands of God for

their own tradition and our own embracing of the tradi-
tions of men to the neglect of the commands of the Lord?

Our goal today should be to be more conformed
to the image and likeness of Christ than our predecessors were, by not continuing in their ill-fated pursuits.
This will mean parting with some of the ideas we
currently adhere to. This will not negate our predecessors nor us for having operated under the ideas and
perspectives that they have given us. Many fear change
because of uncertainty in the future that change
brings. Others fear change because of the present
comfort in the status quo. We should look at change as
an odyssey. Discovery should enthrall us and give us
energy to move on with God. This will necessitate being
humble on our part and continuing to open ourselves
to a continued revelation from God. The question is:

Do we have the humility to admit our denial of
problems in the church due to a political focus and the
shared responsibility in cooperating with the wrong
thinking?

Do we have the humility to make change when it
is easier to sit back and let others do it or just stay with
the crowd?

The Bible tells us that wide is the way that leads
to destruction and many are those who follow in that
way, but narrow is the way that leads to life and few
are those who walk on this path. This is true in all
human activities in life; people like to follow the crowd.
Are we those kind of people? When a captain of a
oceangoing oil tanker realizes his vessel is off course, it
takes about 25 miles to turn the ship off its present
course and get it heading in the right direction. Inertia,
the power of a moving mass, continues to push the

ship in the same direction it was heading even though countermeasures are being exacted to change direction. In the same way there is much momentum, or *thought inertia*, in the body of Christ in this country on this issue of politics in the church. The approach articulated herein is not going to be popular. Thus this "thought inertia" is going to press hard against anyone who wants to change. Those who do not have the humility, grace and fortitude to stand up and chart a different course will be quite outspoken against us. It is not easy to stand against the tides of the times but we need to stand up. The people of God have always had to stand against incorrect thinking and actions. Sometimes that will mean standing up against the direction of the organized church as did Huss, Wycliffe and innumerable others.

Are the institutional organizations that so many call "the church," so perfect that they do not need to change anymore? Think again!

The organized church is not closer to God or more attuned to Him than ever before, but rather the opposite. There is sure and certain degradation from what Christ set in motion.

Read The Bible With New Eyes

One of the things we can begin to do differently relates to reading the Bible without a grid of theological ideals in place. Instead of accepting what others say about a text we can begin to listen to God and find His heart about the application of the Bible in our lives. We no longer have to accept the twists of interpretations that have been hatched over the years. The Bible interprets itself through the help of the Holy Spirit, not some commentator or theologian.

In the list of giftings and offices in the NT church there is no such thing as "theologian." We have given far too much place to this tradition of having others do our thinking for us. We can understand the application of scripture to every situation in life, by God revealing it to us through a relationship with Him. Any true relationship with God must include communication as is natural to all relationships. Circumstances, premonitions, fuzzy feelings, or even high-powered people who "speak for the Lord" cannot be a substitute. We have the Holy Spirit who inspired the Word, who will also interpret the Word, living in us. There is very little else we need. According to the modern lean on theology and commentary writings* in the church today, it would seem that many of us would rather lean on a relationship with a person who wrote about the Bible than the Person who wrote it Himself.

Jesus once made a comment to the Pharisees that gives us a concept which comes in handy to our discussion of taking a new direction. Jesus was answering their questions about divorce. He told the Pharisees that Moses had given the concession of divorce because of the hardness of the Jews' heart. But he continued, "from the beginning it has not been this way," (cf. Matt. 19:8). While this statement may seem insignificant to us, we need to consider its importance. The principle within this comment is this: if we want to see how something should be done, go back to the beginning and see it as it was designed. We will see the intent and the purity of the original essence of what God intended for the church when we go back to the

*Footnote: There is a place for commentary but we do not hear as much in the church today about God showing us a greater understanding than Matthew Henry, or some such other individual. Who is quoted in services concerning further insights on the Bible? This says much about our theology and beliefs. Either God is muzzled by a closed book or we have no intention of listening if He does speak.

beginning when Christ started it. This is one of the missing keys in the modern church in America today, we are so far from the simplicity of what God wanted for the church.

Seek Truth

What has happened in church up to today is that people have added to truth. How does one add to or build on truth? Pastor Richard Wurmbrand, who was introduced before, gives us the answer:

"God is 'the Truth.' The Bible is 'the truth about the Truth.' Theology is 'the truth about the truth about the Truth.' Fundamentalism is 'the truth about the truth about the truth about the Truth.' Christian people live in these many 'truths' about the Truth, and, because of them, *they have not 'the Truth'*. Hungry, beaten and doped, we had forgotten theology and the Bible. We had forgotten the 'truths about the Truth,' therefore we lived in 'the Truth.'"[2]

Today, we live so far from the truth because we have added to it so much, and thus it resembles 'the Truth' very little. In fact it is not the truth, it is only the vapor of the truth. Zinzendorf was credited with this comment about truth, "As soon as truth becomes a system, one does not possess it any longer." This systemization of truth as a tradition was the major defect of the Pharisees. In like manner the organized church in the Middle-Ages, and even in the church of our day, has stooped to this same problem because of the continual lean on systematic theology, worship systems and institutional structures. This has been a darkening effect on the church since the time of Constantine up until the "radical reformers" of the 17th century. It has left an indelible mark on the church even today. We think and approach much of our work today as a direct hand-me-down of the mindsets that came into the church from the beginning of the Dark-Ages.

The early church did very well in advancing the Gospel, up until the early part of the 4th century. It was leading up to this time that leaders of the church organized it into a more institutional organism. This change, along with other historical events, placed a different emphasis on: God, Government, and the identity of the church. Many years later Luther became the catalyst for a sweeping reformation in the early 1500's. Yet he did not go far enough. Nothing changed between the Catholic view on the relationship between the church and the state in Luther's view. Even though great changes have been made since Luther, still the greatest changes are yet to come. This is why we have been given incorrect views and ideas. The people before us have tried to recover that which was lost in the mar-riage of the church to the state under Constantine and all that was added from then up until Luther.

Today the church is in a similar shape to where it was before the Reformation: having a basis in tradi-tion instead of God's leading. Certainly, much has been restored to the church of what was before Constantine. This has come about by way of the intervention of God, through willing servants in the church down through history. However, if new problems have encrusted the church since the Reformation, what is the difference between the pre-reformation church and us today? One set of problems has been exchanged for another set of preoccupations.

It could be argued that the church is under a greater delusion today than before the Reformation. Luke, in his Gospel, speaks of the casting out of a demon. The demon decides to return to his former place and finds it swept and clean, *but empty*. He, the demon, then brings back with him seven demons, more evil than himself, and the last state is worse than the first. Even if this scenario represents the modern church to a degree, we are not beyond help. God wants us to go back to the beginning to our first love to begin to do those things, which are right and true.

The letters to the seven churches recorded in the first three chapters of Revelation were given at one time to a specific group of people. Yet, these letters are very contemporary to us today. God has repeatedly broken off from the organized church at different times in history to use new groupings of disciples that would do His will. The Reformation did a lot to begin the process of revitalizing the church and making it more able to do God's will, but that was just the beginning. The true church has never stopped coming back to the truth or doing God's work. Yet there is certainly more work to be done. There is always a remnant. In the end God is after a pure bride, not one who is looking out for her own interests, or using other lovers to secure them.

Another Reformation

Many in Christian circles today could not even conceive of the idea of another reformation in the church. Our purpose should not be to recapture the past but rather to observe it and seek the Lord. The greatest part of transforming the wasteland we have created in our minds is pressing into Him: letting go and letting God. God is what put the first century church together. He can do what is needed again in new creative ways if we allow Him. Jesus said several times in the gospels that with man, things are impossible but with God, nothing is impossible. We need to believe and seek His help in our day. At the same time we need to reject what we are holding onto as far as security and purpose.

If the church had a political job it would be, "the formation of a people who see clearly the cost of discipleship and are willing to pay the price."[3] What is needed most in the church today are believers who will wait on God to see what He is doing and cooperate with Him. This would be in contrast to simply trying to clean up society around us so that we will feel more comfortable using it as our playground. This kind of "clean up" is selfishly motivated and destructive in nature, though it does not appear so on the surface.

If we are not depending on God to show us what to do, how can we call this society to live and do differently because of walking in relationship with the Creator, when we aren't even at this point ourselves?

From here, we get into real practical applications of transitioning from activist or couch potatoes into being what Christ had intended for each of us to be: soldiers of Christ in His Kingdom. Being a soldier of Christ is the balance, activism or couch potatoism are the extremes. Many would take the words "soldier" and "fight" to mean that our struggle is physical. However, we need to find out what our fight is and how to engage it. We need to stop feeling a sense of accomplishment in our divergent activities, while we think we have been doing what God wants, when we are only doing what we want instead.

THE LIFE THAT IS PLEASING
TO GOD IS NOT
A SERIES OF
RELIGIOUS DUTIES.
WE HAVE ONLY ONE
THING TO DO,
NAMELY, TO EXPERIENCE A LIFE
OF RELATIONSHIP AND INTIMACY
WITH GOD.

– Dr. Richard Foster –
Celebration of Discipline

13

Seeing Our Struggle Correctly

In recent years much has been written about our struggle as followers of Christ. Some books deal with the suffering our struggles bring about. Others deal with various views of "spiritual warfare." This section will deal with our struggle as it relates to the relationship of the body of Christ to the society around us. Struggle will come into play not only as different worldviews converge but additionally as we begin retiring ideas that are not congruous to our role as followers of Christ. Much of the confusion over political activism in the church relates to what the Bible says over and against what believers incorporate into their views/ actions, based on what they *think* the Bible says.

One reason for this derivation is that scripture sometimes gives us what would appear to be contradictory teachings on any number of subjects to include Church/State relations. Because of these apparent paradoxes, (scripture saying two different things about the same subject) groups have tended to embrace one side of the paradox claiming it to be "the gospel" while leaving the other part dormant. Let's look at two such instances evidencing how scripture can be misapplied in people's actions because of taking one side of the truth over and against incorporating both sides.

In the OT there are many prophecies concerning Christ that depict a conquering hero. Still, there are many others depicting Him as the suffering lamb. Both are certainly true but the Pharisees ended up murdering their Messiah because their error was due in part to having made applications from only half the prophecies concerning Christ, rather than all of them.* This example illustrates the fact that people will commonly use only parts of scripture to support their actions rather than all that it tells them.

A second example of scripture seeming to contradict itself hails from NT texts. Matthew 18:15-17 tells us if someone sins against us that we should go to him and reprove him. Yet compare Matthew 18 to I Corinthians 13:5, where we are told "love never takes into account wrongs done" nor gives offense, how do we reconcile these seeming contradictions? This is just another of many examples where believers could embrace one side of the whole truth that is offered in scripture.

All is meant to give examples of what C.H. Spurgeon once called "parallel truths." This gives expression to the situation where various texts could seem to be oppositional to one another. Yet, in reality they are merely flip sides of the same coin. They are meant to balance each other creating stability, thus they are equally important. One way to think about this reality is to consider the expression "truth in tension." This concept can be illustrated by a turnbuckle, see: figure-1 on the following page. To describe a *turnbuckle* it has two components: a metal frameᴬ with opposing internal-threads on either end and eye-boltsᴮ or threaded rod which are commonly installed in these threaded holes.

---

*Footnote: The Pharisees were also jealous of any attention being given to Christ by the common man, because it could have implications on their cultural power.

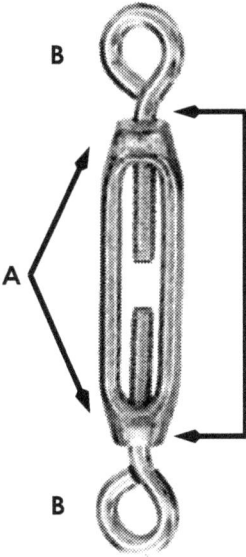

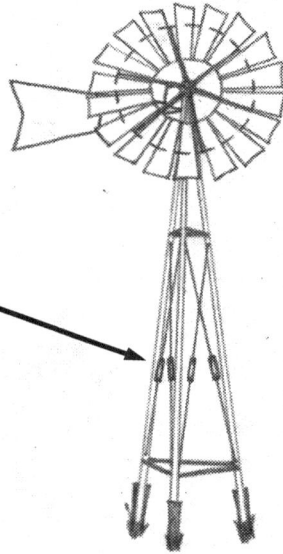

Figure-1   Figure-2

When the frame is turned clockwise either side is evenly pulled inward. Turnbuckles were commonly used on certain windmill designs, such as in the illustration of figure-2 above. The legs of the windmill were connected at the top and fastened to independent foundations at the bottom. Turnbuckles were some-times connected to parts of each leg between the top and bottom, interconnecting the legs. This added strength and stability against torsional forces caused by high winds.

In the same way many truths in the Bible are parallel like the legs of the windmill. However, if we do not include all that is given to us in the Bible on each subject, i.e. the tension of interconnecting truths, (spiritual turnbuckles) instability and weakness are inescapable. We can have all the texts concerning one side of a truth and still be out of balance because we haven't incorporated the other aspects of truth. Employing all aspects of truth gives us the same thing spiritually as turnbuckles give to the windmill: strength and stability.

In everyday living most of us want permanent one-way answers for life and its obstacles. Resistance to change gives evidence that the church also has this general predisposition of leaning on one-way permanent answers. "People of Institution" in most churches resist change not because it is wrong but because it will cause them strain on a personal or corporate level. If they embrace change they also must develop new ways of dealing with life and ministry. This is one reason why there are distinct schools of theological thought, differing political parties and an ever increasing number of denominational groupings.

Sometimes humankind chooses not to adapt to a problem or circumstances. At this point there comes a split in the group. Those who are open to change or those who won't change are made to leave so that the remainder can maintain their status quo. The thinking within the group that won't change is maintained along rigid systems of thought that naturally stave off any adaptation. This approach makes being led by the Holy Spirit impossible.

Now we will look at an area of humanly developed rigid approaches (i.e. permanent one-way answers) which has become a hallmark of the religious landscape in this country. Reference is, of course, being made to the political action of the church in this country. There are two major approaches to this issue. They tend to view each other as "action" and "inaction." The most preeminent idea in America on politics and social issues today is that of "action." The majority of the "action" advocated by the various think-tanks is aimed at people and institutions. There is little precedent that would support this approach if we consider all the Bible has to say. But this problem has never deterred the activist nor the theologians that encourage them. This tendency was noted by another author who wrote, "what astounding lengths do theologians sometimes go in their ambition to find biblical warrant for their own ideas."[1]

It seems that many would merely look for just enough scripture to justify their actions, rather than studying what the whole intent of scripture might be regarding the issues they labor over. If all scripture were weighed, regarding the issue of political activism by the church, there would be clearly another approach indicated than the one being bantered around so much today.

This is where we need the Word of God to pierce through the fog of human thinking and speak off the pages of scripture to become the arbitrator over such things as seeing our struggle correctly. The political-action people tend to embrace one grouping of scriptures (for their permanent one-way answers) while ignoring and downplaying many other texts that would point to another approach. The other camp embraces another group of texts and is derided by the "active" believers for supposedly sticking their heads in the sand and becoming reclusive from the dirty old world. Obviously, neither of these views are balanced.

Converse to the human tendency of rigid approaches to life and obstacle, Christ dealt with many similar interactions in diverse ways. He did not use the same approach in each instance of healing, evangelism, or even responding to certain types of people. It is interesting that Christ used different means with regards to the same situation. Why didn't Jesus respond in the exact same way all the time? The Bible is completely silent as to any specific reason. Yet Jesus said that He was following what His Father was doing and saying. Jesus commented to this effect on three occasions in the Gospel of John, (*cf.* 5:30, 6:38, and 8:28-29). This is directly opposite of the systematic preconditioned responses of most people in the modern organized church.

Concerning our struggle, there is no doubt that we are to struggle or that we are in a struggle. This is why we need to get our minds straight so that we are working in the right direction. What does "our fight is not against flesh and blood" mean? It is this question that we shall endeavor to answer. At first we can say that we should not see the world or its events from the perspective of mere flesh and blood anymore, because these are just shadows of the whole truth. But this is just the tip of the iceberg. As the next few chapters unfold we will see more of what scripture says about our relationship to the society around us.

Some Background

The OT represented the physical-world Kingdom of God. OT Israel was the plan of God. He set it aside as a nation to be His own as part of this covenant. Man always had the ability to choose good or evil. Thus, it wasn't long before this option put a monkey wrench into what God set in motion. Israel was to be the Lord's representation in the world. It was to be a "*type*" (a representation) of what God was going to do in the future. The history in the OT not only gives us the typology of how God's Kingdom is to be lived within a surrounding world. It also shows us that Israel failed to be the light God intended at that time because they rejoined the world in so many ways that it ended up destroying her. God's intentions for Israel in both the active and passive sense are clearly indicated in scripture. The OT is the only real and objective history ever put on paper. God has preserved it so that all mankind can observe and learn.

At a specific point in time, Jesus enters into the theatre of human existence as a man. He came in the "fullness of time," meaning in the fullness of man's futile living even with God's desires and provisions being plainly evident and demonstrated. Jesus instituted a new covenant that also had *a nation* as a part of the plan, (*cf.* Matt. 21:43). The Kingdom in this new covenant was not a "physical-world Kingdom" as it had been in the OT. Jesus came to institute a new Kingdom, not of this world, but one which all men from every earthly kingdom in this world may choose between the two spiritual realities of this life.

The NT was to be the beginning of a spiritual-world Kingdom. Just before His crucifixion, Jesus said, "my Kingdom is not of this world," (*cf.* John 18:36). Paul reiterated this fact in another text saying, "our citizenship is in Heaven" in Philippians 3:20. Prior to Jesus' comment about this unusual Kingdom in John 18, He prayed for us that we would not return to being part of the world, as would be a tendency, (*cf.* John 17:12, 16).* Living in a physical world while being dedicated to a spiritual Kingdom seems to be a hard concept for the church to grasp.

The kingdom of God that Christ spoke of was to be a reality in this physical world but it was never to be bound by geography, religion, ethnicity, earthly culture, or any other human trappings that normally separate people into groupings. What Jesus said and did in the NT was an extension of the typology that had been established in the OT. Israel was once again a "*type*" of that which was to come. And Paul continually drew comparisons from the OT for what God intended in the NT.

A cursory reading of the Gospels shows that what Jesus set in motion was so outrageous at that

Footnote: Look what the disciples did shortly after the crucifixion in John 21:2-10, they went back to their "old lives" being part of the world. In John 17:11-12 Jesus said He was "keeping" the disciples. What was He "keeping" them from? This keeping wasn't just spiritual, it was also in the sense of keeping them engaged in His Kingdom and from going back to being like the world. Left on their own, even for a short time, the disciples went right back to being mere men amongst the world.

time it was hard for even His disciples to believe. They all misunderstood! They were still stuck in the physical world mindset as is evident through their desire to set Jesus up as King and to defend Him by the sword, (*cf.* Matt. 26:49-55). To a great degree, Jesus' intentions are still unbelievable to the organized church today. Instead of wanting to throw off Rome as the disciples wanted in their day, in our day we want Jesus to help us take over society and make it do what we want, what we think He wants.

In our modern era we do not break with society when we come to Christ. This parallels the disciples before Pentecost. There was no difference between the disciples and the Jewish society around them, other than who they were hanging around with. In similar comparison there is very little difference between Christians today and the secular society around us, as Barna and others have documented. Yet, after Pentecost disciples were both notably different than *regular society* and there was a definite struggle between the cultural institution and the disciples that never stopped throughout the pages of the NT.

This struggle the disciples faced was never about the control of society as modern activists have tried to revisionistically interpret it. This struggle was about the presentation of a competing option to the world's society. Concerning the modern church, our errors, such as being indistinguishable from society, are not so much out of ignorance due to a lack of information. Our errors begin with that we are still sold to thinking as the world thinks and so we miss God's intent. This is why we need to know God's voice and read the scriptures without allowing theology to cloud our minds. Many times, what God is doing is inconceivable to the minds of men, even regenerated man, "My thoughts are not your thoughts..." (*cf.* Isa. 55:8).

The institution of this new Kingdom "not made with hands" presents a sense of "otherness" to the physical kingdoms in the world around us. If we live this "otherness" as we are supposed to, it will bring on a huge struggle. The nail that sticks up is going to get pounded down. Generally speaking cultures are fairly uniform in values and ideas, especially regarding religion and social protocol. One fellow wrote that societies are "*sacral*," meaning groups of people are "bound together by a common religious loyalty."[2] When followers of Christ propose a new concept that is not of this world's system, the world will struggle against us. Yet even through this "struggle" the world will plainly see the option of light and truth that they do not have.

When we live the gospel we introduce an un-wanted competition to the world's society. The contrast between the vast darkness of the world and our community of light sharpens. When the gospel is preached and people of society come into truth, society then becomes composite. There are now ideas compet-ing for a "following" for lack of a better expression, (*cf.* Acts 5:12-18; 16:16-40 (esp. 35-40); 19:20-27). This will always produces struggle in the physical world, yet it is in this ensuing struggle that we [followers of Christ] are not to fight in a physical sense.

Our Struggle Is **NOT**

Paul begins his discourse in Ephesians 6:10-18 concerning our struggle, by telling us what it *is not*. Our struggle is not against *flesh and blood*. This means people, human institutions or anything of human origin. These are not our enemies, nor are we to offen-sively engage them as such. To see people or organiza-tions as an enemy is to miss the very essence of the message of Jesus and His gospel of the Kingdom. It also is preamble to all sorts of physical and political wrangling. The evil that people may do to us is not against us but against God and His purposes, because we are His representatives, not His defenders.

If our struggle is not against flesh and blood, then we cannot struggle against whatever is happening in the world through the ways of flesh and blood. It is simple; if we use the world's techniques we will get the world's results, period! We cannot march on Washington or "jam the switchboards at Capitol Hill" and expect to get different results than the world gets when it fights against flesh and blood using the same means. If we use politics the way the world does, we become "just another special interest group to be appeased by politicians."[3]. There might be short-term victories, but should we settle to win a few skirmishes in the temporal while we forget the war about the eternal?

As evidence that our struggle is not against flesh and blood, Chapter 2, *"Stupid Is As Stupid Does"* articulates in great detail the score card of conservative political groups that have failed in their attempts against flesh and blood. Conservatives have used the same ideas and approach as the civil rights fighters employed in trying to accomplish their purposes. While the conservatives' work culminated in direct access to a President, even this accomplishment has done little to achieve the conservatives' original goals.

If we take a minute to consider that abortion has not been stopped but expanded and deviated in the most heinous ways—that the homosexual agenda has burgeoned into a federal case under the conservatives' watch—that the cultural understanding of marriage has come under attack while the conservative has been fighting their self titled "culture wars"—that euthanasia [doctor assisted suicide] has also come into play as another social issue, all of a sudden we see an ever widening battle with no complete wins on the conservatives' original platform. Yes, stem cell research has been curbed [certainly not stopped] and partial birth-abortion has been banned, and the defense of marriage act has been offered up. But the core issues of the conservative platform are still alive and well. Nothing has been put to bed!

The conservative movement has not gained so much as the first mile of their original objectives. Cal Thomas realized this fact several years back and wrote a book: *Blinded by Might.* He wrote, "Today very little that we set out to do has gotten done. In fact the moral landscape of America has become worse."[4] Because the Religious-Right has engaged flesh with flesh, they have relegated themselves to *trying* to plug all the holes on a dam that is continuing to disintegrate. After 40-years their approach has not worked and it never will. If the foundations are destroyed, what can righteous men do, King David asked in Psalms 11:3.

We cannot fight against the world the way it fights with itself. We need to be the "Holy-Other" to the world around us.* The enemy knows this and will bring physical trouble against us as we seek to walk in the way Christ told us to walk. The people and institutions of this world are not the problems, neither is straightening them out ours. Sin is the problem and lack of relationship with God is another big problem for mankind. Political engagement or domination will not fix either of these problems. If we concentrate on our real job, the "culture wars" the church is currently embroiled in will change for sure.

Our Struggle **IS**

While the prior section dealt with what "our struggle is not" it is clear from Ephesians 6:10-18, that we are to engage in a specific struggle. Our struggle is

---

*Footnote:** This is not advocating that we are "god" or that we are somehow holier than the world around us. This is noted to promote the fact that we are God's representatives and that we have much to do in becoming truer in our representations of Him. Of course, this a vulnerable and uncomfortable position but it is none-the-less still true.

against, "the *rulers*, against the *powers*, against the *world forces of this darkness*, against all the *spiritual forces of wickedness in the Heavenly places.*" Paul lists four entities that we are to struggle against. The list is cumulative, meaning that each successive nouns build towards the overall meaning of the passage.

Again, it is clear that the object or focus of our struggle is not the physical world. Dean Sherman wrote, "Satan is working through mankind to do his business on the planet. And God is working through mankind to defeat the enemy. This is what has been happening through the ages."[5] We are to be God's tools in the work of spiritual warfare on this earth. If we concentrate on the physical, we will repeat the totality of church history from the time of Constantine until now, where so-called "Christians" used manipulation, coercion, force and even torture as means of gaining complicity and "conversion," i.e. "culture change." The mindset of conservatives would repeat most wars in history, as well as all kinds of dissension and every evil that could be imagined.

Is that what we really want?

More importantly, is this what God wants?

In addition to our text in Ephesians 6:10-18, Paul also wrote, "For though we walk in the flesh, we do not war according to the flesh, for the weapons of our warfare are not of the flesh, but divinely powerful for the destruction of fortresses," (*cf.* II Cor. 10:3-4). It becomes very difficult to agree with this scripture and walk in the way of the religious activist.

So, if our struggle is against spiritual foes, how is it to be fought by other than spiritual means?

How can the religious conservative political action crowd incorporate this scripture into their support basis and practice?

The conservatives are left to use the other parts of scripture to support the way they choose to engage *a struggle*, (not to be confused with our actual struggle). They either have to leave this text out of their considerations or they must twist it to make it fit their way of doing business. As we consider the II Corinthians 10 text further, in verse 5, Paul goes on to say, "We are destroying speculations and every lofty thing raised up against the knowledge of God, and we are taking every thought captive to the obedience of Christ." This text can be twisted to say that we should go after the aberrant ideas of society to force them into compliance with our God's truth. Actually this text refers to being introspective in the church in controlling the natural human reaction or rejecting lies which may provoke us to act in non-sanctioned ways. This text is not to be applied imperialistically towards an unregenerate society.

Notice that Paul did not take any campaign to any governing agency or faction. He did appear before such, but only under their means of force. Only then did he deal with these human structures of leadership and even at that he engaged the situation from the perspective of continuing to spread the gospel. Paul was not ever caught up in worldly defined issues or structures as a means to his end. Paul concentrated on our job as disciples and because he stayed "in the pocket," to use a football analogy, and an entire empire was being dramatically changed the way God intended in a mere 25-years. Something is remarkably different about Paul's approach than that of the modern church. The miraculous results give a strong indication as to which approach God is behind.

When we side-step the systems that the enemy uses to establish and maintain control over people's minds, while providing the light God intended, we are going to be in for a full-blown engagement. When we offer to the people of this world a different option of commitment and loyalty than the world's systems and ideas, we are coming against these systems of the world by being the "holy other" (the Kingdom set apart within the world). As we walk the way of being this "holy other," engaging problems at the spiritual level rather than the physical, we will be undertaking our struggle properly.

There is, on the part of the enemy, a real effort to destroy us and make us worthless against him as well as being worthless for God's purpose. If the enemy can intimidate us and/or if he can get us to sidetrack from God's plan then he has succeeded and we have failed. God has given us the means, through what He did on the cross and His resurrection, to go on the offensive spiritually. The only things that regulate what we do in our mission are the Holy Spirit and disbelief.

Our objective in life is to plant seeds and nurture them so that believers sprout as a result of the Holy Spirit's work. This will only happen as we do our work of spreading seed, watering and tilling the ground. Our struggle is to do what God has commanded us to do in light of the resistance from the physical world to do what we've been commanded. Our struggle is to stay on the narrow path of our lot in life and not be swayed into doing mere "good works," as defined by the world, or be deterred through intimidation, complacency, distraction or laziness. Our struggle is within us and yet all around us as well. Nevertheless, be of good cheer, He who has overcome the world is in us and we will overcome, IF WE ABIDE IN HIM!

Further Thoughts & Applications

Beyond the objective truth of what our struggle is and what *it certainly is not*, there are a few things that we should consider. To start with, one writer put it this way: "Christianity grows alien to its essence when it is made into law for those who have been merely born instead of reborn."[6] Trying, emphasis on TRYING, to legislate morality is all that government has to offer the activist. Government can never deliver morality amongst the people it governs. It can at best only hold anarchy at bay while regulating business, law and trade through restrictions and guidelines. This is both God's intended purpose for government and the limits He gave it. We are sinning to put our trust in men that sit in governance and try to legislate morality. Equally we are sinning to try and dominate the political process and try to make men act morally by enacting more stringent laws. We can register our voice morally on referendums and voter initiatives. But to trust in princes to do the work of the church is a denial of who we are as the Kingdom of God amongst the kingdoms of men. God did not advocate this approach even in the OT, (cf. Ps. 118:8-9; 146:3, Jer. 17:5-8).

The only determining factor that can positively affect any nation to go beyond external government force is when its people get right with God! Otherwise, people do not have the means to overcome their nature as "monsters of iniquity" as revivalist preacher George Whitefield used to say. The world's solutions to problems [education, external force or peer pressure] are a far cry from real change brought about by transformation, regeneration, reconciliation and hope. These can only come from God and that is why we need to tend to our business. We are God's only representatives and the business of winning souls for Christ and discipling them in God's way is our job. This is influence not domination. This is Christ's way, not the doctrine of demons.

The problems the modern church sees in society are mostly spiritual in nature. The physical manifestation we see is evidence of greater problems, we should not be attacking the manifestations. God says that the world is the way it is because it does not know Him. Can the government fix that? No way! You cannot put a governmental Band-Aid on spiritual problems, it will never work! Every problem mankind has is rooted in relationship issues. God has given the follower of Christ the sole work of reconciliation not only between men but more primarily between God and man.

Currently, we are leaning away from true evangelism, reconciliation and discipleship, and instead investing in radical forays into civilian living. God shows us in the Word that the problems of the world should be dealt with, but because we are citizens of Heaven there is only one way to deal with them and that is God's way. The devil has a hay-day provoking disciples to address the world's problems in the ways of the world. When we do that, we lose. God has said this approach will not work, but many believers seem to believe a demonic logic more than they believe the scriptures or listen to what God is saying. When people in the Bible did what God said to do, exactly the way God said to do it, they always prevailed!

Are We Listening To God?

Consistently, Jesus said, "Let him who has an ear to hear, let him hear," This phrase is used in one form or another some 16-times in the NT. That means God has something to say directly to us today about the application of His Word in this world wherever we live. It also means that we should be listening. This is why the Bible is called the "living word" of God. While it was spoken to men and written down, God still speaks through it today. While the Bible is but mere words on a page they come to life for each of us as God reveals their applications to us. If all we do is read the words of a book, albeit the Bible, never allowing God to speak, we downgrade what Christ taught to being nothing more than religion. Religion in essence is a belief system centered on man's limited, selfish perspectives of interpreting what he wants the way he wants because it suits him.

Given this analysis we become no different than the Moslem, Buddhist or any religious group that observes writings to promptly go their way and apply them in their lives by their own strength. If we continue to do the things of the world and do not pay heed to God's ways and His voice, we can expect to repeat history and the cyclically tides of man's inhumanity to other men. We must come to the place where we are willing to take our hands-off the flight stick of life and give God what is His.

Corrie Ten-Boom, the Dutch saint who hid Jews during WW II and was imprisoned for her work, had this to say afterwards. "I learned to hold everything with a loose grip because it hurt when God had to peel my fingers away." We have to be of the mind that we just might lose the living that we've enjoyed in this land. What is more important, our comfort and relaxed way of existing, or His purposes?

Questions To Consider:

Haven't we become like the Pharisees of old who sought to try to restrain the downward spiral of culture and society through the devices of men?

Didn't Jesus condemn the Pharisees because they left God out of their equation in their belief and practice of "purity"?

Aren't religious activists of today doing the same thing as the Pharisees in trying to stem the moral free-fall of a society though political means?

Why wouldn't Jesus condemn the actions of those today that are following the ways of the Pharisees?

We need to adopt the mindset, birthright and heritage that are ours in Christ. We should not be like Esau who sold his birthright for a mere bowl of soup. Esau's bowl of soup is for us our Kingdom citizenship that we've so far traded off for a sub-identity in this society. We think this sub-identity gives us sustenance, meaning and purpose. It has nothing actually to do with who or what we really are. The late Keith Green said it right when he sang, "You love the world and you're avoiding me."[7] Jesus said, repeating what was said through the prophet Isaiah, "This people honors me with their lips but their hearts are far from me." Let's not be this kind of people anymore. Let's throw in the towel on assumed identities and a masquerade that transforms the truth into mere religion. Let's stop being just another amongst many and begin to be the "holy-other" God intended us to be.

14

What Are We More Than Others?

In the early 1980's the late Gordon Petersen of Souls Harbor Church in Minneapolis, Minnesota preached at my home church. His text was a very short one, (*cf.* Matt. 5:46-47). What was taught from this text has stuck with me to this day. Gordon broke the application of that section down into three points: What have we, What do we, and What are we, more than others? I want to borrow from that teaching; what we do and what we have emanates out of who we are.

As mentioned earlier, much has been written about the believer's identity in recent years. Still many struggle with who they are and what it means in a practical sense. To my knowledge, very little of what has been written deals with who we are not. This is also a defining point in understanding our nature and identity as followers of Christ. Most books that I have seen from Evangelicals dealing with the believer's identity, stop with the mind. Many do not address our identity in respect to the Lordship of Christ over the believer's life. None of these books deal with the aspect of our coming into a new citizenship. Many of these books go no further than encouraging good thoughts or removing ideas that do not feed "a positive self-esteem."

The modern approach to "our identity" makes it very difficult to plug in what the Bible actually says about our identity. Unfortunately, much of what the Bible tells us about this subject gets tucked away into the "closets" of the theological house in which many of us take up residence. What the Bible says does not always neatly fit into the way the theology we've accepted causes us to think. Therefore, our identity becomes just a thought, a mental assent, rather than a practical and livable reality.

To illustrate, let's assume that we know a little bit about electricity because we have read some "how-to" books. Now, what about being thrust onto a job site as a fully trained electrician? If we are not electricians, meaning having been trained in a 4-year journeymen program, it's going to be next to impossible to do such work. Despite our basic knowing a little bit about electricity, it would be unlikely that we could live out "the being" of what an electrician does. Spiritually speaking, we need to get some training in what have become hidden aspects of our identity so that we can live out of our identities the way God intended. Because of the theological overlays we've accepted, our true identity is about as real to us as *Jack and the Beanstalk.* If we don't peel away all the overlays that we operate under we will never be able to plug in the practicals of *"what are we more than others."*

We are no longer what we were before we came to Christ. Scripture is very clear about that! Modern believers have been handed a watered-down gospel in which "total change" stops at mental assent* after a few bad habits and a few rough edges have been smoothed over. Our modern tendency skirts the all en-

*Footnote: Mental assent means that we agree with a teaching intellectually but we allow it very little if any sway in our lives. In some places "conversion" means that you have grunted affirmatively concerning a few theological statements.

compassing nature of what a "total change" really involves. While we still live in this "physical" world our nature and identity must be totally changed according to the conversion that Paul taught. We can't be, by the very nature of what God does in us through salvation and sanctification, what we were before we were raised up anew in Christ. *God transforms us, which means total change.* When electricity is converted from AC (alternating-current) to DC (direct-current) the electricity becomes totally different. If we were to plug in a DC motor to an AC wall plug, the motor would be destroyed in an instant. Because of transformation or conversion, we are no longer what we were in the same way AC current is no longer DC current once it has been converted!

This far-reaching concept of total change is a special problem for believers in this country. We still commonly think of ourselves as far as where we are from –an American– rather than whom we have become through conversion–Christ's followers. We have our hands on the plow but we are looking back. As I have read the Bible, in light of the relationship between church and state, I've found awesome accounts in scripture that deal with our identity, or who we see ourselves as, e.g. "what are we more than others." The next few chapters will bear witness that the way we have come to think in the modern church, because of activists' compounding* interpretations of scripture, is quite opposite of what the Bible teaches.

Initially, we need to break off from the ideas of nationalistic mindsets that exist in the organized church. Our identity is not based upon a nationality but rather on a relationship with God and His Kingdom. If we would resist seeing ourselves as Americans

*Footnote: "Compounding" means adding to the already molested understandings and ideas about what scripture means. Theological twists, history and the human tendency towards the degeneration of pure truth are all precursors to the activist's further tweaking.

per-se through a crafty retelling of history or some theology, then we will not be pulled into the kind of misplaced diligence we see with the Religious-Right "Christian" political agenda. Biblical examples of how nationalistic views get in the way of what God wants to do can be found in Acts 15:1-12 as well as Jonah 4.

Multiple allegiances will always cause problems in ministry. This is why all followers of Christ today need to break with the unbiblical ideas of patriotism and a nationalized citizenship. These ideas do not belong with people who are claiming to follow Christ. In II Corinthians 5:17 (NKJV) Paul writes, "Therefore, if anyone is in Christ, he is a new creation (some versions say "creature") *old things have passed away; behold, ALL things have become new."*

How many things have become new in this text?

Investigating this text further is the key to the real picture of "who we are more than others." Volumes could be written about this text without exhausting its meaning or impact. And because this scripture's meaning is so vast we need other texts to help interpret its meaning. One specific application of II Corinthians 5:17 can be found in Philippians 3:4b-11.

> 4b If anyone else has a mind to put confidence in the flesh, I far more: 5 circumcised the eighth day, of the nation of Israel, of the tribe of Benjamin, a Hebrew of Hebrews; as to the Law, a Pharisee; 6 as to zeal, a persecutor of the church; as to the righteousness which is in the Law, found blameless. 7 But whatever things were gain to me, those things I have counted as loss for the sake of Christ. 8 More than that, I count all things to be loss in view of the surpassing value of knowing Christ Jesus my Lord, for whom I have suffered the loss of all things, and count them but rubbish *in order that* I may gain Christ,

9 and may be found in Him, not having a righteousness of my own derived from the Law, but that which is through faith in Christ, the righteousness which comes from God on the basis of faith, 10 _that_ I may know Him, and the power of His resurrection and the fellowship of His sufferings, being conformed to His death; 11 _in order that_ I may attain to the resurrection from the dead.

This text has epic implications concerning the subject of church/state relations and a believer's identity. Paul starts by referring to confidence in his flesh, meaning who or what he was by way of ability, birth, nationality, achievement, social stature, or any other human trapping by which he could draw attention to himself. Just prior to this text Paul condemns the "circumcision"* for placing confidence in being Jewish. The significance of this text is that Paul equates all he had become before Christ to manure! Lets look at what Paul articulated what "confidence in the flesh" meant concerning himself and how each item relates significantly to our modern situation.

Chart-B

Compare Paul's Day To Our Own (cf. Phil. 3:5-6)

Paul	Modern Day Equivalent
1. Circumcised on the 8th day	Baptized/Dedicated
2. Covenant People	American
3. Benjamite (Extra Special)	Our Denominational Affilations
4. Hebrew of Hebrews (Special Lineage, Genealogy)	Family Identity (Who's Who)
5. Pharisee (Pure)	Systematic Theological Stand
6. Zeal to Protect God	Political Activism (Defending God and Country)
7. Blameless According to the Law	Model Citizen

Footnote: "The circumcision" were teachers who mixed Jewish rituals with the teaching of "faith in only Christ" for salvation.

There is more to this larger text of Philippians 3:4-11 than the majority of modern believers allow themselves to see. Grammatical details in the original language tie preeminent importance to an identity change as a part of salvation! In verse 8 Paul uses the phrase "in order that" (a conjunction) which ties a restrictive clause (a condition) to a *result*. In other words, if you don't meet the condition you can't have the result. This may be a tough pill for some to swallow but let's look at it further.

The Bible simply does not teach the cheap grace; that is, grace that has no conditions or restrictions placed on its being granted. Cheap grace, the conditionless-gospel that is taught so widely today, is nothing short of easy-believism. It has rotted the fiber and strength out of the message of the gospel! The Bible teaches that grace is freely offered to all, but at a very high price. That high price is our very identity, and the right to run our life independently of God.

In the Philippians text reproduced on page 165-166 the conjunctions as they occur in the Greek are underlined.* This text emphatically expresses that we cannot gain Christ, know Him, or attain to resurrection from the dead or have the fellowship of His sufferings, *until or unless* what we were in the past is rubbish to us and treated as such in our lives.

The words *"in order that"* in vs. 8 are translated from the Greek primitive conjunction *Hina* (Strong's #2443). The word "Hina" joins a restrictive clause to the definition, purpose, or result of the preceding condition. In other words this verse is saying, the definition of a follower of Christ is one who suffers the

---

*Footnote: Some underlining in the text on 165-166 are implied conjunctions in the Greek in this passage. However, in verse 8 there is no question in the Greek as to if there is a conjunction.

loss of all things to include an earthly perspective of themselves, counting it as rubbish. Richard Wurmbrand articulated this same idea in his own way, as he personally came to recognize the magnitude of what it means to follow Christ. He wrote, "A man who has lost, in addition to his beloved ones, all his belongings, his health, his reputation, and *his liberty*, must seek these things in the Bible. He will surely find more than he has lost to include the conviction of the irrelevance of the things lost."[1] Wurmbrand's conviction wasn't an attempt at giving lip-service to a novel, idealistic interpretation of scripture. He paid dearly for it with 14-years in Communist prisons suffering continuous torture!

Coming to know Christ is limited in this text by the Greek. The condition in this text has to have been God's intent because this clause is used the same way *157* additional times in the NT.

If every other use of this phrase throughout the entire NT is a condition, why would this understanding of the phrase suddenly change here when it is specifically tied to salvation?

Are we trying to support a theology or are we sincerely seeking to see what God is trying to say in this text?

We cannot identify with Christ if in our minds, and thus in our living, we are like what we were before we came to Christ. Think on this just a bit. To put it another way, we cannot identify with Christ if we still think we are what we were! Proverbs 23:7a says, "For as he thinks within himself, so he is." All is to say, how we think of ourselves is very important! We still live in the world as we did before we came to Christ. Yet now we are to be "in Christ" and thus out of the world's way of thinking. We cannot have or be both, "in Christ" or "in the world," or we will be double-minded, unstable in all our ways, (*cf.* Jas. 1:4-8, 4:8).

Christ was our example when He gave up who He was in order to become our propitiation—the sacrifice in place of us, (*cf.* Phil. 2:5-9). Christ becoming our forgiveness and High Priest was contingent on Him giving up all that He was in Heaven, as well as who he was on earth (a man with a free will), to be what God intended, (*cf.* Heb. 2-5).

What Are We More Than Others, As Believers

In correlating to II Corinthians. 5:17 and Philippians 3:4-11 we reviewed earlier, there are other scriptures to help fill in the blanks of who we are and what we are to be doing. The accompanying list is not exhaustive but it is meant to show an extensive range of work and capacities we need to attend to as followers of Christ. Each point will be accompanied by texts so that you may look further into each for yourself.

For each aspect of our identity and work, the enemy of our souls has provided either inversions or opposites that counterfeit God's design. The enemy is not stupid, so many of these "substitutes" do not appear to be huge departures from God's way. But let us not be deceived by cunning or by our own simple-mindedness to think that any differences articulated in the next few pages lie only in semantics.

We are *Ambassadors*, "Therefore, we are <u>ambassadors</u> for Christ, as though God were entreating through us; we beg you on behalf of Christ, be reconciled to God," (*cf.* II Cor. 5:20).

The inversion of this aspect would be a *lobbyist*.

The lobbyist represents a group of people to a larger system of power in an attempt to acquire money, power, favor, attention or a change in policy. Unwittingly this approach empowers and encourages a government to be selective and preferential in its policy focus which can be a bane as much as it could be a boon to the lobbyist and the group he represents. Another problem for the lobbyist is that he is prone to being used by politicians without the politician reciprocating on the lobbyist's interests. This is a real picture of the conservative movement. Even with good intentions the activist is nothing more than a lobbyist, i.e. just another special interest group that politicians can choose to placate when it serves their purposes.

An Ambassador represents his realm to another realm. He is empowered by his own citizenship and is no more or no less significant because of how the realm he is in treats him. Because an Ambassador represents something outside of the realm he is in, he can offer to that realm what he has from his own realm. He doesn't need to profit by offering what he has, nor is he profited in his offer being accepted. Therefore he is both an objective and unbiased giver in what he does. As Ambassadors of Christ, we can offer truth, peace, meaning and purpose.

> We are *soldiers*, "Suffer hardship with me, as a good *soldier of Christ Jesus. No soldier in active service entangles himself in the affairs of everyday life,* so that he may please the one who enlisted him as a soldier," (*cf.* II Tim. 2:3-4).

The opposite of the soldier is to be a *civilian* person. Civilians enjoy the freedoms of a political realm but are not under compulsory duty to it, other than to obey the laws of the land. They can go about their own interests with minimal commitment to civic duty. They are not duty bound to serve the state

The soldier's role could be misunderstood and so there is a need to clarify. Of the six times in the NT where this word picture is used, the concept is not one of defending but one of discipline, readiness and duty. We do not have to defend God, but we do need to work at self-discipline, and we have to see our duty of being totally under God's direction. The modern church seems to be allergic to these aspects once they are pointed out and oblivious to them otherwise.

> We are *servants*, "Let a man regard us in this manner, as servants of Christ, and *stewards* of the mysteries of God," (*cf.* I Cor. 4:1). This is of course said of Paul himself but is also true of us. We are servants of God to the world.

The opposite of servant is a *co-equal.* Co-equals compete with others of the realm, protecting their own personal interests. They often dominate and marginalize other people in seeking to exploit state granted rights to their advantage. Earthly realms offer rights to all and man, being the monster he is, seeks to get all he can. Even for the man claiming Christ, if he maintains an identity in the world, he will participate in this survival of the fittest exercise.

The servant role can be misunderstood to mean someone should be a carpet on which everybody is to wipe their feet. Converse to this idea, "servant" is a strong word that means giving and taking care of needs from a strong position of endless provision, i.e. God. We can serve others because we are empowered, better equipped, we have better provisions and we have been fulfilled in Christ. We do not need to acquire any of these things from the world. What we have cannot be taken away, therefore we are in a strong position to be giving just like Christ, (*cf.* Mark 10:45).

We are *light,* "For you were formerly darkness, but now you are *light* in the Lord; walk as children of light," (*cf.* Eph. 5:8-11). "*You are the light* of the world," (*cf.* Matt. 5:14a).

The opposite of light is *darkness.* Darkness refers to being spiritually unclear. Religion is burdensome and confusing. Sinners are spiritually blind; why pile on heavy moralistic duties that are confusing without having first offered them the source of being moral? Conservative political activism is a derivative of spiritual truth that is being foisted on a larger public. This public is vastly ignorant of who God is, yet conservatives want people to be moral without knowing God, the only means by which anyone can be moral. What could be more unclear than this?

Light by contrast quietly shines out into the darkness and is not overcome. There is absolutely no need to make noise because the difference between light and the darkness of the world surrounding it is unmistakable. Our light should be encouraging as in "light at the end of the tunnel." Our light is not to be used as a cruel search and destroy tool. Our attitude makes all the difference in the world as to whether the world is being drawn to the Christ we are lifting up or driven away by the religiousness of being forced to be moralistic, through a political process albeit an attempt to "uphold righteousness," without knowing the basis for morality.

We are *not our own anymore,* "*You are not your own.* For you have been bought with a price: therefore glorify God in your body," (*cf.* I Cor.

6:19b-20). Glorifying God in our bodies applies to what we do with our life, not just what we ingest.

The opposite of this aspect is *self-actuating*, the ability to do what we want, when we want because we want. There is an imperialistic self-absorption in the essence of the activists' approach, nobody else counts except what they want. Add "religious purity" and a mob to the elements of self-actuation and you have the makings of an Inquisition or a Crusade. This approach falls in direct line with the worst in history that can be attributed to people calling themselves "Christians."

When we are "not our own anymore" we are God's. We are not part of the surf of the world which aimlessly washes back and forth. We are not marginalized by all the hubbub or the magnitude of the world. When we are being directed by God we will accomplish significant things. But these will be different from what the activist can touch. The activist haggles with the world over its goods and services. The follower of Christ dispenses to the world what it cannot have other than through Christ.

We are *Priests*, "You also, as living stones, are being built up as a spiritual house for a *holy priesthood*, to offer up spiritual sacrifices acceptable to God through Jesus Christ...But you are A CHOSEN RACE, A royal *PRIESTHOOD*, A HOLY NATION, A PEOPLE FOR God's OWN POSSESSION, that you may proclaim the excellencies of Him who has called you out of darkness into His marvelous light," (*cf.* I Pet. 2:5, 9).

On this point an inversion has been made that has affected the church for 1600-years. The idea that there is a *"higher-calling"* and *"lower-calling,"* or *priests* and *laity,* in the church is a bankrupt idea when we look at scripture for support. This concept has allowed the vast majority of believers in history to settle back into belonging in the world because they are not considered to be "*higher-calling*" or *priests*. This mindset is totally against all that Christ taught!

The kind of priests Peter wrote about represent Christ to the people outside of the Kingdom of God. They aren't to represent an institution to a local mutual admiration society! Peter called all followers of Christ to be priests. There are no "non-priests" in God's Kingdom.

> We are *citizens of Heaven,* "For *our citizenship is in Heaven,* from which we also eagerly await for a savior, the Lord Jesus Christ," (*cf.* Phil. 3:20). Citizens of the Kingdom of God, not the world! We have responsibilities as citizens of Heaven.

The opposite of a citizen of Heaven would be a "*citizen of the kingdoms of men.*" Followers of Christ who have not made this jump from one kingdom to another will focus only on the here and now. They will constantly be manipulated by the ebb and flow of politics because of their hope to use it. The citizen of the kingdoms of men is representing God only through the systems of men, and this is a mighty poor platform from which to work.

While we live in the world our very nature and identity must change in the conversion process. We no longer dance to the world's tune as do the unregenerate. Once we realize that we are really citizens of Heaven, we become the alternative the world both wants and hates. But they cannot obtain what we are and have through any means other than through Christ, whom we represent.

We are *salt*, "You are the *salt* of the earth; but if the salt has become tasteless, how will it be made salty again? It is good for nothing anymore, except to be thrown out and trampled under foot by men," (*cf.* Matt. 5:13). Too much salt will kill, too little will kill as well.

The opposite of salt is *the common aggregate of society*. Once salt loses its taste it becomes good for nothing, other than to be trodden under the feet of all other men in the world. When we use the world's techniques and play their game their way, we become one of them. As the church has leaned on politics to do our work, influencing culture, we have become a very small fish in a very large ocean. Politics marginalizes many more than it truly helps.

There is also a common inversion to the imagery of *salt* within the modern church. To many today, salt has come to mean *preservative*, which it is from one perspective. The only problem is that scripture NEVER depicts salt in this way! In keeping with the connotation of salt the conservatives have drummed up, they contend that we should "preserve" society with our brand of piety. They believe they are doing this country a favor, saving it from certain judgment.

The NT depicts salt in the imagery of seasoning or flavor. Besides sustenance, food is a comfort to people and seasoning adds flavor that would not ordinarily occur in that food. Life is natural to all men and a follower of Christ can bring seasoning to the natural life of mankind. This addition can bring comfort to others and draw them towards the Kingdom, just like light. Our work as seasoning makes us stand out from the crowd. Seasoning is subtle but still very definable to those who want to discern its presence.

We are *aliens* and *strangers*, "Beloved, I urge you as aliens and strangers to abstain from fleshly lusts..." (*cf.* I Pet. 2:11-12).

The opposite would be *fellow citizens,* which we covered earlier under *"co-equal."* There is a common inversion of the concept of "aliens and strangers" that is much a part of church history. Some have unscripturally come to think of "aliens and strangers" in the sense that we drop out of the world totally, as some kind of recluse or holy colony, staying away from the dirty rotten world. This is clearly unscriptural because it contradicts Christ's prayer that we would be available to the world, (*cf.* John 17:14-18). How can we be a light to the world if we are never in their presence or if we severely limit our contact with them?

A surprising point about all the examples and direction Christ and the Apostles set forward in scripture about church/state relations is that they did not depict images of dominance, superiority or belonging within the world's system. Yet every one of the inversions and opposites which the conservatives employ are dominating and very much inclusive in the world's ways. God's way presents a picture of duty, purpose and service outside of the world's way of thinking.

As we can see from the list above, our plate is already pretty full. Most conservatives would argue that they embody all these scriptural aspects in their efforts. This would seem plausible if you did not consider any of the unflattering details about their activities and failures recorded in Chapter 2, *Stupid Is As Stupid Does.* Otherwise their claim to being the embodiment of all that we should be as followers of Christ would be believable. In truth the fundamental essence of each of the aspects of our true identity and work cannot be fulfilled in the applications for which the conservatives have pilfered them.

Some Questions To Consider:

How does one act as an Ambassador, in representing His Kingdom to another, if he first fails to understand that he is an Ambassador and secondly that he belongs to another kingdom than the one he lives in?

If the Ambassador has to surrender the essence of the values of His Kingdom to the state he hopes to present to, through their systems of protocol, of what good is the Ambassadorship and of what good is the message or its presentation?

As far as Soldiers go, at what point do we become renegades from our own army? Is it when we pursue things that we have not been directed to pursue? Or is it when we cease to accomplish the objectives we should be fighting for because we have engaged in a distraction rather than the cause? Or even yet, is it when we alter our ammunition to the point that our ammunition is indistinguishable from that which the world uses?

Are we citizens of Heaven in how we approach this country, being respectful of others' wishes and considering others before ourselves?

Or are we "rights" based, operating selfishly because the rights granted to us by the state are overlooked or curtailed in the course of where this country is going?

What is motivating us? Are we trying to maintain a place to hang our hats or are we going about God's business, which has an eternal impact? Does God motivate us or are we motivated by selfish reasons while we try to couch our work in "trying to uphold righteousness"?

Our responsibility is to show the world Christ and His Word by allowing them to see truth in us. In pursuing the objectives of the political activist we can only try to maintain a thin cover of morality ourselves. Attempting to get people (non-believers) to be moral and calling it "upholding righteousness" is not moral or what Christ called us to do. We need God to guide us or we will be led by our feeble understanding of what we think He wants. With few exceptions this fleshly attempt ends up being self-serving, not God-serving.

This chapter is just a start down the path of rethinking the involvements we have taken on. Our list of *who* we are is a good place to begin because it shows us so many parts that must be lived out in the King-dom of God. This phrase, Kingdom of God, is a detail we should spend more time studying as well. It is also part of who we are in identity. It is these concepts that have not yet made a total impact on the church in America.

PATRIOTISM/NATIONALISM ARE
MECHANISMS OF NATURAL
HUMAN CULTURE.
THESE TWO 'ISMS" FEED THE
HUMAN MIND WITH DIVISION,
PREJUDICE AND MOST EVERY KIND
OF EVIL EVER DEVISED.
WHEN WE COME TO CHRIST, HE
DOES NOT HELP FEED THIS
HUMAN NATURE.
JESUS DOES NOT GIVE ROOM IN HIS
GOSPEL FOR SUCH BECAUSE THEY
NO LONGER MATTER.
JESUS HAS REQUIRED US TO DIE
TO THIS WORLD AND TO BE RAISED
IN NEWNESS OF LIFE, THOUGHT,
EXISTENCE AND REALITY WHILE WE
ARE STILL IN IT.

– Timothy L Price –

15

My Kingdom Is Not Of This World

This title is a sound byte from a conversation between Jesus and the Roman Governor, Pilate, (*cf.* John 18:28-40 esp. vs. 36). Pilate was not one to be trifled with and those times were politically tense. Yet, notice what Jesus said to this Roman authority. Christ's words could have seemed either seditious or crazy. This was an interesting dialog, which raises the question of why it was recorded in scripture. Better yet, what is the lasting significance of this dialog? Was the dialog a space filler or does it contain material we haven't noticed yet?

This dialog between Jesus and Pilate came at the end of a three-year ministry. During this period Jesus attempted to convey His purpose and objectives to the disciples as He trained them to continue in His ministry. While they understood Jesus to a limited degree, their own dreams and aspirations for Him, to be a conquering hero for Israel, got in the way of them ever fully understanding Him. They were transfixed on the physical and were very much nationalistic.

The Jews, meaning the religious leaders of the nation, held similar ideas to the disciples about the

Messiah. Having grown up in this traditional mind-set the disciples carried these ideas right into their work and relationship with Christ. In the Garden of Gethsemane, Peter even drew a sword and used it. He was ready to fight for "the kingdom," which in his mind was to be a physical reality (*cf.* Matt. 26:51, John 18:10).

Even after the crucifixion the disciples asked, "Lord, is it at this time You are restoring the kingdom to Israel?" Obviously, they were still holding onto this same paradigm of the Messiah being a conquering hero for Israel, (*cf.* Acts 1:6). This evidences their nationalistic hope. Peter and the others thought that the Kingdom of Israel and the Kingdom of God were one and the same. Thus the disciples missed much of the meaning behind what Jesus said, because they filtered everything they saw Him do and say through preconceived ideas they continued to carry from their upbringing.

Today, not unlike the pre-Pentecost disciples, we also carry preconceived ideas into the Kingdom as well as into our reading of the scriptures. Even though we have the entire Bible, we also miss specific applications such as the kingdom of God amongst the kingdoms of men. Thus, we walk in the footsteps of the same faulty thinking and actions as the Pharisees and disciples. Today it is unbelievable how many believers think we should be taking "dominion" over this country. Yet we can't find any example in Christ Himself. Paul repeatedly said, be imitators of me and/or Christ. This means to do the same things they did.

Does the passage of time since Jesus' life form the basis for another dispensational chop* out of what parts of the Bible are supposed to be for today?

*Footnote: "Chop" means to take out or do away with. Dispensationalism is a philosophy that breaks history down into segments of how God supposedly dealt differently with men. This view has become an easy means for this kind of believer to de-emphasize practices that they don't like.

How can people divorce Jesus' and Paul's life performance from who we are and what we are to be doing today?

One argument attempting to explain the lack of advocacy for political activity in the life of Christ or the Apostles, is that their lives had specific roles thus they could not divert from these. A second argument is that neither Jesus nor the Apostles had the "stewardship" opportunity of a representative government so they could not have been an example in this way.

The problem with the first line of rationale is it intimates that in our day we *do not* have specific roles* to carry out concerning God's work in this world. Thus, we are "free" to take on other engagements that might seem more important. The second supposition is purely situational. It puts circumstances in preeminence over the Bible. We're limiting our understanding of scripture through a modern secular protocol rather than looking at any situation the world throws at us from the vast perspective of scripture. In either case we end up nulli-fying scripture's applicability in our times, or stretching it beyond its intended purpose.

Political involvement is not forbidden in the Bible. At the same time, Christ and the Apostles (the examples we claim to be following) never engaged in such activities and there were reasons why they didn't. Perhaps the primary reason Jesus and the Apostles did not bother with the political arena was because their kingdom was not of this world. Their actions were consistent with the concept of living as Ambassadors from another realm. By contrast, the ideas of activism are consistent with being part of the world's system and wanting it to give us whatever we think we deserve.

*Footnote: The reference to specific roles for Christ and the Apostles and non-specific roles for us today, relates to the "Higher/Lower Calling" heresy addressed on pg. 174. It is thought that since we have a lesser role in the kingdom we can do whatever we desire instead of the specific things we have been commanded to do by scripture, or a specific direction given directly by God.

Can we see the stark difference between Christ and the modern mindset here? Activism is temporal in its focus; Christ and the Apostles were purely eternal in their focus.

Jesus had the perfect opportunity to be clear about His intent on this earth when He stood before Pilate. His words could not be understood that He was trying to institute a theocratic physical world entity, i.e., "Christian-Nation." If Jesus' intent was to establish an earthly kingdom in a geo-political sense, He would not have been brought before Pilate. He also would have acted much differently throughout His life and work before this time. Point being, Jesus was not in the least bit interested in political "dominion." He was offered a form of dominion, gained through illegitimate means, by the devil in the wilderness and promptly rejected it. He will be given dominion in the legitimate sense because of His obedience in dying on the cross, (*cf.* Phil. 2:7-11).

So why has the church in America fallen for the trap in the ideas of political "dominion," when the God they claim to follow did not? Modern believers are either ignorant and deceived or they are not following the same God as the one in John 18.

Consider the dialog between Jesus and Pilate further. Jesus did not answer some of Pilate's questions but at other times spoke at length concerning truth and His identity. Pilate did not flinch in view of the political ramifications of what Jesus said, but he listened. He did not take Jesus to be some streetwise crackpot. Yet, he understood Jesus in ways the Jews, the disciples and even modern believers don't understand. Pilate did not pursue the exact meaning of Jesus' comments concerning His Kingdom, because he knew it to be deep and costly: commodities in which Pilate would not trade. Ultimately, Pilate gutlessly politicked his way out of making a high intensity moral decision. Based on what he knew, Pilate did the more expedient thing of turning Jesus over to a democratic-mob to be executed. It is interesting to note that Jesus was murdered by a small *democracy,** i.e., rule by popular opinion.

The Kingdom Of God

The concept of the "Kingdom of God" is found throughout the pages of the NT. The word "Kingdom," as it relates to the Kingdom of God/Kingdom of Heaven, is used more than 130-times in the NT. Jesus made 90 of these mentions Himself. These two terms are used interchangeably throughout the Gospels as well as the Epistles. The number of references make this concept of "the Kingdom of God" one of the major topics of the NT.

Just what is the Kingdom of God and what does it mean to us?

How would the Kingdom of God amongst the kingdoms of men change our ideas about a supposed "Christian-nation" and our ideas of nationalism?

Jesus used many illustrations and parables to depict elements of "the Kingdom." Jesus used the phrase, "the Kingdom of Heaven is like," or "to what can we compare the Kingdom of God." So in the chart below let's look at some correlations between earthly kingdoms and the Kingdom of God. In any kingdom, there must be sovereignty and an area of domain. There are rulers and subjects. There are heirs to the power as well as servants. There is a value system and protocol; this is how things are culturally done. There are also cultural objectives. These aspects are what comprise a kingdom and differentiate it from others.

Footnote: In the crudest sense this mob was a democracy. It acted as a democracy with popular opinion winning the day.

Chart-C

Earthly Kingdom	Kingdom of God
1. Ruler	Jesus through the Father and Holy Spirit
2. Sovereignty over land and law	Absolute Sovereignty over all of creation
3. Domain-Land or Area	Peoples: identity, lives, hearts and w ork
4. Levels of pow er-agencies	Offices in the w ork of God
5. Protocol	Respect for all men, and honor for authority
6. Political posterity	Heirs to God's Kingdom in Christ
7. The w orking class	Servants
8. Dominant Cultural Values	The Fruit of the Spirit
9. Motives and cultural objectives	Giving to Christ w hat He is w orthy of
10. Citizenship	Living out our destiny in Christ

These aspects of the Kingdom of God identified in the chart can be found in scripture. Each aspect needs to be responded to in our lives. We can't just take what we want of the Kingdom of God, like *hors d'oeuvres* at some party. It is an all-inclusive deal. In the same breath, we cannot serve two masters. We can't have one leg of our identity in the world and the other in the Kingdom of God. Christ said we will either hate one and love the other or vise-versa, (*cf.* Matt. 6:24). There is no way to escape this choice. Yet, many believers earnestly try to have it both ways: be a citizen of an earthly kingdom, and oh, by the way, be citizens of Heaven. Most believers would be quick to add this second association in passing, but are very slow in being able to articulate how they go about their Heavenly citizenship. An earthly belonging is much more doable and real to the average believer.

What has been taught to most western Christians is a *syncretism* that allows the believer to cope with life "in the world," while only making a passive mental change in awareness about God. Forget practical applications of a Heavenly citizenship. A heavenly citizenship is more of a biblical wall decoration than anything. By the way, this is not the gospel and if it were, we would not be discussing church/state relations today. There would have been no church, no Reformation, and no ecclesiastical history. The sect of Jesus would have died within the generation it was founded, having no impact on the world. It would have been no different from a minor religion that flashes on the screen of human existence only to end up as a footnote in some textbook.

The Error Of An Imbedded Earthly Citizenship

The truth about our citizenship and our identity in Christ wars against much of what we've learned in our upbringing in this culture. In America, there are dozens of organizations focused on instilling citizenship in the earthly sense, from childhood on up into the adult years. There are groups like FHA, FFA, 4-H, Boy Scouts, Campfire and Girl Scouts and so on. On top of this, various "Christian" organizations do the same thing. It is amazing that "Christian" organizations teach secular citizenship when Paul says, "For our citizenship is in Heaven, from which we also eagerly await for a savior, the Lord Jesus Christ," (*cf.* Phil. 3:20). It is no wonder the church is in bed with the politics of the society of this country. Why shouldn't it be, given the church's strategic departures from the Word of God?

Why do so many "Christian" organizations teach earthly citizenship instead of citizenship in the kingdom of God ?

Isn't the answer to this question solid evidence that we are making the same associations between God's followers and a nation, creating a "Holy Nation" mindset just as the disciples thought of Israel?

Peter wrote, "But *you are A CHOSEN RACE, A royal PRIESTHOOD, A HOLY NATION, A PEOPLE FOR*

God's OWN POSSESSION, that you may proclaim the excellencies of Him who has called you out of darkness into His marvelous light," (*cf.* I Pet. 2:5, 9). Peter's text dovetails a comment Jesus made to the chief priests and elders of the people, (*cf.* Matt. 21:43). He said, "Therefore I say to you, THE KINGDOM OF GOD will be taken away from you, and be given to A NATION producing the fruit of it." The nation Peter and Christ were talking about has nothing to do with an earthly kingdom like America, especially as we ponder Christ's statement to Pilate in John 18:36. It is difficult to see how anyone could make associations between America and the Kingdom of God. Such attempts should defy the imagination of anyone well-grounded in scripture.

In Chapter 1, *Subjective Thinking In The Camp,* we discussed how the imprinting of our formative years fosters a natural resistance to ideas that appear to be "new" to us, even if those ideas aren't new at all. Since we also tend to be *Syncretistic-Thinkers,* as discussed in Chapter 7, *Mis-Identity As A Motivator,* there is little motive to ever think about the potential for inconsistency between what we believe from scripture and the way we live. Motivations to rethink ideas we've been given by society are further pacified in that much of what we have been taught by secular entities is also buttressed by church teaching. Thus, many believers glibly go along with the status quo, because they know nothing else. When we seriously start talking about "to what kingdom we belong," and "my Kingdom is not of this world," most believers are scared to death. This seems totally new, and very intimidating to them.

The ideas of nationalism, ethnicity and earthly citizenship for the believer have no foundation scripturally. We must downplay scripture's authority in order to continue being motivated by these concepts. The concepts of belonging, politically and nationalistically, are allowed to be parasitically brought right past the cross, into the church. The modern church's teaching is so watered down that anyone willing to mumble positively in a couple of places is welcomed into fellowship without a word about the cost of discipleship. Nothing is mentioned about an identity change, or about our citizenship being in Heaven.

We are new creations, having a new identity, outlook, purpose and a concept of kingdom outside the common physical world ideas we covered in Chapter 13, *Seeing Our Struggle Correctly.* If we are following Christ and His kingdom, then we must divest ourselves of the theological crustaceans that have barnacled the hull of truth we claim. The Kingdom of God is a finished work as far as God is concerned. There is little else for us to do than bring in those whose time has come to enter. This was depicted in the parable of the king who gave a wedding feast, (*cf.* Matt. 22:1-13). This job is enough for us, yet the politically involved church spends so little time in this effort as we saw in Chapter 2, *The State Of The Church.* God has prepared everything for us in Christ; we are participants in His established work. Jesus said, "the fields are white unto harvest." That means the fields are prepared, grown and ripened, all by God's hand. It is just a matter of going out and bringing in what Christ has already prepared.

We don't have to create a kingdom that supposes itself to follow God's moral laws, by merely emulating a code of exterior morality. We are not part of the world in the sense of citizenship, being motivated by this human connection. We do not have to clean up the world because we'd be embarrassed should the Lord return and find it a mess, thinking we were lazy for having left it that way. We shouldn't want to clean the world up so that we'll feel more comfortable, relaxing in a more moral environment, till He returns. An old gospel song grasps the truth about our citizenship in

Heaven. Its verse reads, "This world is not my home, I'm just a-pass-in' through," (the closing refrain) "and I can't feel at home in this world anymore."

Do we feel at home in this world?

The world is not ours, nor is it our home or playground. We've been commissioned and commanded to evangelize and make disciples of all nations. The church is God's kingdom on earth to do the work of gathering souls and teaching new believers how they should be conforming their lives to Christ once they are brought into the Kingdom. As increasing numbers of true disciples come into the Kingdom, the world will change. This is a by-product of the prime objective of shining the light and bringing in all those who are contrite and surrendered.

Paul spoke of being built up together into a Kingdom. There are many parts and aspects of a Kingdom; someone has to fill in each of those spots. That is where you and I come into play. If all we do is to believe the Gospel with just our minds, we are still lost. The Bible says that God's word is living and active. If we follow God and His Word, we will be active too. But again this "activity" will be much different than the political activity of the conservative activists.

"Well," you say, "what is the difference between the *activeness* of folks in political activism and the *activeness* you're writing about?" Plenty! The motivation and outcomes in conjunction with the action taken, make all the difference in the world. To compare these two forms of "action" is like comparing a bank robbery with a test robbery done by a security agency. Yes, there was a "robbery" in both cases but the realities in each situation are totally incomparable. The activity of the conservative is certainly "involved" physically but it lacks authenticity of scriptural support and is basically selfish. The activity of Christ and His fol-

lowers is and was both scripturally authentic and totally selfless. Conservatism does not enjoy these same
commendations.

We must begin to live from the perspective that
we are a Kingdom unto God: a Kingdom separate from
the world, while still living within the world. We are the
light of the world, yet if we are submerged into the
world's thinking and living we are also sticking our
light under a basket and hiding our light from the
world. If we are sustained by the world's means and
not by God, the world cannot see who God is or what
He is doing. Neither can they see our relationship with
Him. We are to be His flesh and bones, a form of His
incarnation in this world. This is not to be taken that
we "are Christ" as some mistakenly teach. We are a
representation of Him.

*If we are no different from the worldly how can
those of the world see truth?*

The Kingdom of God presents to the believer
the greatest family and fellowship that is possible in
human existence. The Kingdom of God is the greatest
sign of God's work in the world and the biggest stumbling block for the world. Being what God has designed
us to be is not comfortable, but it is what God wants.
We'll fellowship with Christ in His sufferings as we
partake of what He has given us to do in His Kingdom.

Let's get to the point where we can agree with
Christ that our Kingdom (belonging) is not in this
world. Let's begin to think and live out of our true
heritage instead of some recent imposter that feigns the
appearance of significance only to entrap believers into
divisiveness and utter insignificance, counterproduc-
tive to the cause of Christ. 10,000-years from now, it
will make no difference whether we were Americans in
this life or Chinese slave labor. Yet, the ramifications of
making the mistake of basing our lives and worldview

on the perspective of being an American will have profound effects well past 10,000-years. We need to get beyond the world's way of thinking and living and get into the reality that we are the Kingdom of God amongst the kingdoms of men.

16

Comparing Ideas Of Citizenship

Much is said these days about "citizenship" in light of the events of our day. It is said that citizenship begins at the ballot box but continues on from there. Much unlike the way in which citizenship is based in secular and religious circles, we should turn our attention first back to what the Bible has to say about the believer's citizenship. If the Bible delineates the believer's citizenship as being different from the common ideas subscribed to in religious circles, then we ought to pay special attention to what the Word has to say and bring our thinking and living into compliance.

The discussion of this chapter stems from a long text in Philippians 3 that we began to address back in Chapter 13, *Seeing Our Struggle Correctly*. In Philippians 3:1, Paul states that it is beneficial to his readers for him to write the same thing here that he discussed before. Thus, it would seem that Paul's discourse needed to be addressed repetitiously. Yet, even in the regularity in which it was repeated it has been preserved in written form down to our own day. The fact of multiple teachings in Paul's time and at least one remaining to our own day indicates that God is intent on keeping this subject in play not for just the early church but also in our own day.

In the third chapter of Philippians Paul plunges into a teaching where he repudiates the significance of his status and all his accomplishments according to the flesh. Jews in Paul's day commonly justified themselves by recounting their history which made them who and what they were in a nationalistic sense, e.g. God's chosen people. The Jews were proud of their heritage and flaunted it in their tradition of recounting who they were. In the same way conservatives justify themselves by recounting a revisionistic history that gives believers cause, as we discussed in Chapter 6, *History As A Motivator For Political Activism*. Recent history is the place of origin that supposedly legitimizes patriotism and nationalism for believers in this country. And from these two *"isms"* flow the ideas of political activism in order to save that which would seem to be ours. In other words, we give ourselves the same kind of significance as the Jews did by legitimizing our political activities through recounting a history that justifies us in a geo-political context. This practice is a complete inversion of what Paul wrote to the believers at Philippi, (*cf.* Phil. 3:4-11). It is obvious that people today think they have a right to maintain the ideas of nationalism/patriotism and thus an earthly citizenship, *but do they?*

How did we come to think this inversion is right?

The foundation for an earthly citizenship, as being something a believer should fight for, has come to us from a long litany of ideas. It all started when the Roman Emperor Constantine merged the church and state into a single entity. For centuries since, believers bought into this false idea of the church and state being one. From Constantine's time on, conversion was simplified into coercion. Because of Caesar's edict of tolerance and his move to institutionalize it people could see that being named "Christian" was both wise and profitable, thus many "converted." In this new order, under Constantine's tampering, one could not only save his neck by "converting" but he could also profiteer from this newest venture of state business: "Christianity."

Even though we have recovered most of the original teachings on conversion as coming through faith alone, we have failed to deal with a change in identity that used to be part of the process. The country in which one is born continues to be an identity and maybe even considered "property." Compounding this problem even further, democracy is a very welcoming atmosphere that believers can have a voice in. Now there seems to be nothing to resist. The longstanding connection in people's heads between citizenship and identity in a country, automatically desensitizes them to the realities of their true identity and their part in the Kingdom of God. We still think we are part of the world's society and we certainly act as such. One author noted on this point:

> In the twentieth century (as well as many others) we have become accustomed to the fact that in the name of the nation, Catholics will fight Catholics, Protestants will fight Protestants...the charge of blasphemy, if it is ever made, is treated as a quaint anachronism; but the charge of treason, of placing another loyalty above that to the nation state, is treated as the unforgivable crime.[1]

Many believers in this country look at the Puritans and the American Revolution as the foundation of something that is ours, which God specifically gave to us as believers. It seems odd that believers would look at this so recent historical event. There are many other events in history more significant to who we are and what we are to live out, the vast majority of which precede America's founding. Since there is such an influx of modern ideas concerning the believer's identity, finding the original basis for a true under-standing of who and what we are should be major goals for each of us.

In the early chapters of this volume, reference was made to looking at "recent history" as the means of basing significance and justification for our actions. In focusing on recent events, we are robbed of the perspective we'd gain from observing all of history, especially looking back to the church's founding in Acts. If we look only at the near side of history to justify our actions, it becomes easy to think we are correct in our approach concerning our *en masse* political involvements.

If we are going to look at sources outside the Bible to help give us significance, why would we look only to recent historical events?

Do we think we are closer to the truth or have perfected it more in recent years? <u>Think again!</u>

What about the "in between," between the Bible and Puritan history?

If we look at these "in between sources" does the religious conservative mindset of political involvement hold up?

Through simple readings we can see how people of the early church lived out of a different perspective on scripture than we do. When we see concepts taught in scripture and lived out into the second and third centuries, it tends to build a case concerning the purity of their ideas and practice. When these practices disappear off the scope of common discussion in the fourth and subsequent centuries, it should lend to the suspicion of loss. Where did they go? It is in fact this loss of practice concerning the believer's identity, citizenship and the relationship between church and state that needs to be recovered in our day.

Do we think that the early church was a group of unorganized neophytes, muddling around trying to invent something that we have now perfected over the centuries?

To give a snapshot of the way the early church thought about citizenship we can turn to the middle of the second century, about 130-150AD. A fellow named Mathetes wrote an *epistle* to another obscure fellow named Diognetus. While this "epistle" is not on par authoritatively with the Bible, it certainly gives us insights into the way people in that era looked at and expounded on texts of scripture, which we seem to skate right over in our modern readings. Mathetes expounds on Philippians 3:20 very nicely.

From Chapter 5 Of The Epistle To Diognetus

For the Christians are distinguished from other men neither by country, nor language, nor the customs which they observe. For they neither inhabit cities of their own, nor employ a peculiar form of speech, nor lead a life which is marked out by any singularity... But, inhabiting Greek as well as barbarian cities, according as the lot of each of them has determined, and following the customs of the natives in respect to clothing, food, and the rest of their ordinary conduct, they display to us their wonderful and confessedly striking method of life. They dwell in their own countries, but simply as sojourners. As citizens, they share in all things with others, and yet endure all things as if foreigners. Every foreign land is to them as their native country, and every land of their birth as a land of strangers.[2]

The reason for drawing comparisons between this quotation and its parallel in Philippians is to broaden our understanding. We need to see how the early church applied the scripture of Philippians over and against how we've come to misunderstand, if not overlook it, today. What piqued my interest in this letter to Diognetus is that it fit with a larger group of scriptures that otherwise lie dormant in modern views dealing with politics, government and the identity of the believer. This quotation gives us an idea of how people in the early church thought of themselves in relationship to the society around them.

As another part of the changes under Constantine, the church changed its self-perception, function and purpose. Instead of the church being a group where only those who followed Christ by repenting and committing to Christ as Lord made up the body, after Constantine got finished meddling the church was reduced to being a public institution for all people in a given location: a building. Scripture has never supported this new view, yet it became the preeminent mindset for the next 1600+ years with few exceptions. Since the "Constantinian change,"* in the church from the middle of the fourth century, we've tended to see ourselves as being part of the culture around us rather than being separate from the world while existing within it. The early church mistakenly offered up very little resistance against these changes by Constantine.

Carry this change in thinking right into the American Revolution, adding to it the impact of believers having spilled blood for belonging to the state, now we have a deeply ingrained problem. We've unwittingly adopted the views that were handed down to us down

*Footnote: The "Constantinian change" as it is referred to above was when the secular Government of Rome legally sanctioned the church around 325AD. What followed was a merger of Church with State, resulting in the State being the means of enforcement for church ideas and philosophies in exchange for the church supporting the state's will.

through the centuries. And with them came a whole regimen of distractions such as trying to work through societal mechanisms to effect change and letting the government provide a place for us in society. All the distractions brought on by these changes in thinking/ living have kept the church busy and away from being an alternative to the world's societies or spreading the gospel of the kingdom.

Another part of today's misunderstanding of this text in Philippians 3:20 comes from how one word was interpretively translated into English. The word in Greek that "citizenship" was translated from in most modern English versions is: *politeuma* (Strong's #4175). From this word we derive direct correlative words in modern English such as polity or politics. The KJV Bible translated this Greek word into "conversation" which is the only English translation to do so. In all fairness to the King James Bible there were some con-nections between the Elizabethan usages of the word "conversation" and "citizenship," but this detail is lost for most KJV readers other than Shakespearian actors or English professors. Undoubtedly, this mistake in translation has galvanized modern practices over the error of Constantine's change.

In the early church era Rome was the center of the political universe. Not everyone was a citizen of Rome. Being a citizen meant that you were afforded benefits that common people did not have. It might be comparable to a communist party member over and against a peasant in China. While being a "citizen" was not the only status a person could attain in Rome, any other category of person was better than being labeled a person of sedition. When one was culturally branded in this way, death was usually not far away.

In Rome there were many ways to become "seditious." Primary among them was to promote ideas that were exclusive and outside of what Rome itself promoted. This put you first in line as seditious. The world's system and religious institutions have always misconstrued truth to be seditious and subversive if it is not being promoted by them and if the group offering it is doing so in an exclusive fashion. Truth is not something that can be held by a few for the sake of power. Concerning Rome, it was a pantheistic empire but no god was higher than Caesar or the state; this was the state's idea of "truth." When people espoused Jesus as Lord and they affirmed that they wouldn't have any other God before them, this exclusive claim made the followers of Christ public enemy #1 as far as the establishment was concerned.

Believers coming from the Jewish culture in Israel to the fellowship of Christ faced a microcosm of the problems believers faced with Rome. To advocate Jesus Christ was tantamount to disavowing Judaism, the establishment's form of "truth." The Jews, as could be seen at Christ's crucifixion, were fanatical about controlling what was to be believed by the masses. To suggest another idea placed one in the same danger as pursing outright rebellion against the Roman state. Believers were commonly put out of the synagogue for advocating Christ as God, the Savior of the world.

When someone came to Christ it was not some light-hearted whim "to accept Jesus," as it has become today. It was the end of who you were in commerce, family, social status and most other human connections. To accept Christ was to avow an idea that would contradict the state which held that there was no higher god in Rome higher than Caesar. This was the beginning of the forging of "another people," God's "holy other" amongst the world. To espouse Christ as the Messiah for a Jew was to put oneself out of the only fellowship Jews had. Of course, there were exceptions to these violent reactions, but generally you stepped off the deep end when you put forth Christ as your life.

As the original church came together in their common expulsion from the commonwealth of society, before Constantine, they naturally bound together in community. They met from house to house sharing what they had amongst themselves. The common believer did not become reclusive; there was nowhere to go. Earlier in the gospels Christ had stated His intentions for the church, "Therefore I say to you, the kingdom of God will be taken away from you (Israel), and be given to *a nation* (the church or kingdom of God) producing the fruit of it, (*cf.* Matt. 21:43). We were to be a nation unto God, a light to the world, just as Israel was to have been in the OT, (*cf.* Deut. 28:1).

How can we be a light to the world if we are no different than the world around us in what we do or think?

There is a concept in OT Israel and in the early church that we do not understand or apply today. It concerns how we see ourselves in perspective to the world. Israel, even the Jews of Christ's time, saw themselves as totally outside the rest of the world, which they called "Gentile." Jesus wants us to have this same mindset, that there is one church, one Kingdom of God, standing apart from all the kingdoms of men.

How can we deal with this modern trend, of the church being no different than the world around us, if we do not at the same time deal with our citizenship and identity errors?

Generally speaking, citizenship means belonging to a purpose greater than ourselves. It is a collective idea built upon the actions of singular belonging members combined in a group dynamic. Citizenship connotes the ideas of: identity purpose, meaning, duty to cause and responsibility to the group serving that cause.

If citizenship for the secularists begins at the ballot box and continues from there, where does the practical side of our citizenship in Heaven start?

Who talks about the requirements of citizenship in Heaven as they talk about earthly citizenship?

Do the conservatives in the church, who place such an emphasis on earthly "duty" to state, place as high an emphasis on believers' duty to their heavenly citizenship? I don't think so!

The actual meaning of citizenship in the kingdom of God or in Heaven takes some time to sink in for most of us. We are not used to thinking in what appears to be extremism, regarding what citizenship in Heaven means. The concept of citizenship in Heaven for the average church person is as abstract and foreign as Picasso's art. While we readily agree on a mental level with the text in Philippians 3:20, the practical level seems to be much tougher. Speaking in physical-world terms, very few people carry a "dual citizenship," meaning an equally recognized citizenship in two countries. When we step into the spiritual realm there is no such thing. One is either a child of the light or a child of the darkness.

Usually when people move from one physical place in this world it involves a change of location, scenery, familiar places and so on. When we change kingdoms spiritually, we aren't changing locations as we would in the physical world as we go from one country to another. In an accepting society there is no resistance to one making a spiritual change. And so the change between kingdoms is hardly noticeable, both to the believer and to the world around him. Hence in today's culture, the change between physical and spiritual world realities is hardly recognizable.

Many in the modern church think that since there is little resistance from the physical realm for changing their allegiances to the spiritual realm, that it is wise to settle back into the physical world and carry a "dual citizenship." One reason we do not feel the heat of making a decision for Christ as did the early church is because the modern church is not teaching the same things. The early church understood being citizens of heaven to mean the community of the church become a competitive entity to the world's society. The church provided; work, sustenance, counseling, money, help and togetherness outside of what the world offered.

Since we have never left the world's society in our practices as believers, the difference between the sinning society and the church is no longer obvious. The worldly society we supposedly came out of (only not really, it's just a head-trip), is still who the modern church is today. Any new citizenship is as unclear to the new "convert" as it is to the sinning world around him. The church cannot be an ambassador to the society around it. We are still one with society looking to the state to do everything we should be doing while we sit back in our pews wasting our lives, going through repetitious words and meaningless rituals which we call church services.

Just what are the expectations of our being citizens of the Kingdom of God?

In Matthew 21:43 Jesus' comment to the Jews was that they had not produced the fruit that was expected of them. Implicitly, Jesus is telling us that the production of fruit is a measure of expectation for the church as well. Chapter 2, *Stupid The State Of Things in the Church in America* shows us that we lack much in this area.

Is the fruit Jesus referred to the Fruit of the Spirit, or is there more to His meaning than that?

While one cannot discount the evidences of the

Spirit in our lives, e.g., the Fruit of the Spirit, it would be impossible to park the total intent of what Christ said on this one aspect. Fruit in the biological sense is the means of reproduction and viability of any type of plant life. While evidence of God in our lives is without comparative, neither is spiritual reproduction [fruit after our kind]. Every living specie has the means of reproduction or it simply becomes extinct. Reproduction for every believer, bringing in new converts and discipling them, cannot be excluded by any interpretation that is biblically accurate. This is just one aspect of our newly found citizenship.

The fellowship of His Suffering is an expectation of our citizenship, (*cf.* Phil. 3:10). Suffering is something that is not taught in today's church because it is something we cannot identify with. Suffering* is something we are allergic to in the West. However, Jesus said that it is expected that we would suffer for Him. One aspect of suffering is being hated by the world. Today, the non-believing world generally speaking does not specifically hate Christians, especially not in democratic countries. So, does this mean that man has reformed since the time of Christ and various texts are no longer applicable? (*cf.* Matt. 24:9, Luke 21:17, John 15:18, 17:14, Phil. 1:29 and II Tim. 1:8). Or does this modern departure from a sign of following Christ imply that we are preaching another gospel today—one in which the world is not pricked by our lives or testimony, where no controversy stirs over whose kingdom one is in?

Another aspect of our citizenship in Heaven has to do with having the mind of Christ, (*cf.* I Cor. 2:16,

Footnote: While we speak of "suffering in the world" this does not equate to being spoken against or some other soft form of treatment to being persecuted. We should not confuse ill-treatment due to arrogance or our own stupidity with true persecution. Few in the western world speak of persecution from the perspective of knowing its depths such as people in Communist or other repressive states. It is an insult to those who have suffered so greatly to compare most things religious persons in this country face to that of other places or other times in history.

Phil. 2:5 NKJV). If we had the mind of Christ, we would be doing the things Christ did and what God is doing now, (*cf.* John 5:30, 6:38, and 8:28-29). Can we say that we are following what we see God doing, as Jesus did? If we have the mind of Christ, our interests would be those of Christ's and we would focus our work along what He shows us to do. We have to ask ourselves whether Christ was an American or even a world citizen or if He would seek the favor and complicity of the world's halls of power? The answer to these questions should be obvious. How come we feel that we must seek government recognition of righteous living and the complicity of an unbelieving society through laws, amendments and such? It is precisely because our citizenship has been prostituted to another that any believer would seek for a citizenship from this world. The church does not yet see what it really is.

Another aspect of our citizenship in Heaven would be unity of purpose and existence. Since we have broken ourselves down into quibbling sectarian groups over scraps of truth rather than embracing collective truth of the Bible, we do not yet have the camaraderie of being citizens of Heaven together with believers worldwide. We allow the policies of the government we patronize in false worship to divide us against brethren in other countries. We first let the world's ways divide us nationalistically and then we divided ourselves ecclesiastically. This is a further clue that we have departed from the whole gospel.

Citizenship, specifically "heavenly citizenship," is a tremendously under-emphasized subject in the modern church. Most Christians would generally agree to all the aspects we covered thus far; however, few ever go past mental agreements to functionally belonging to the kingdom of God though fulfilling citizenship responsibilities. This "extreme" is left to the "super-spiritual." This delegating of our God-mandated duty kind of resignation comes from the concept of *Higher-Lower Calling*, as covered in Chapter 14, *What Are We More Than Others*, which is another product of Constantine's meddling; this is not biblical! We each have our cross to bear and function to live out both towards the world and within the fellowship of Christ. We could continue to explore aspects of who we are as citizens of Heaven. I think it would be better if we continue this discussion in the next section as we talk about how these aspects can be employed. It is one thing to understand the meaning of something and quite another to be able to apply it.

17

How Then Shall We Live?

In the last chapter we dealt with the meaning of our citizenship in Heaven; in this section we will address the practicals of application. How did the Apostles and early Christians live out their new citizenship in the world of their day? We must get past the establishment mentality of the institutional church and face the fact that we are out of touch with the reality of who we really are. The abstruse for us today is getting over the fact that society has become indifferent to us in large part. But the indifference of society towards us can change as we come to terms with the truth that we are a Kingdom unto God and begin to reassert who we really are through performing our citizenship duties.

One of the realities of the early church's approach to living out its heavenly citizenship was through *compositism*. These early Christians probably never saw it this way or had any such term to describe it. Compositism refers to a society that is made up of several different ideas mainly pertaining to religious loyalties. This had nothing to do with the fellowship of the church. It merely expresses that they were willing to exist alongside society's people who believed very differently. Early believers did not have the dominating mindset of being an institutional establishment that we do today. The fact that there are more believers in society today does not excuse our attitudes of establishment thinking, i.e., that we are the cultural dominant. It was never expressed in the NT that we should embrace this mindset, to where we expect the secular society around us to placate us in the public square.

Right alongside of compositism in the early church was another idea: influence. This simply means that the desire for change in society only comes through the demonstration of truth in our living it before society. Society would learn truth and want to emulate it when they saw it, not when they were browbeat about it. Leonard Verduin, in his book *The Reformers and Their StepChildren,* put it this way;

> "It is implied in the NT vision that Christianity *would not* be a culture-creating thing but rather a culture influencing one. Whenever the Gospel is preached human society becomes composite; hence, since culture is the name given to the total spiritual heritage of an entire people, there can never be such a thing a "Christian Culture" (this would be the same as a Christian-Nation for those of you in Coral Gables); there can only be cultures in which the *influence of Christianity is more or less apparent.*"[1]

Conversely, the ideas of Romans, Jews and almost any religious group or culture has been "contigutive," meaning that there were no genuinely competitive options for those under the care of the governing body. Though Rome was a pantheistic, state-run religious system that had many "gods," this system was still the government's. And Christians were seen to be a threat to the control and power exerted through the state religious system. Believers offered an exclusive teaching and society to the world around them. They lived peacefully alongside various belief systems but did not conform to them; they became the composite in society. Then they lived to be an influence for the Kingdom.

When the Constantinian change was allowed into the church, it was an epic event similar to the forbidden fruit episode in the Garden of Eden. The problem in America is that the conservatives have fallen into believing and living as the Romans, Pharisees and other religious groups before them without realizing it. They have come to think erroneously that society and government should reflect and support their views, e.g., an inclusive religious/social philosophy. The only difference between modern-day believers and the merely religious animal of society is that in the case of "Christians," following the true God of the universe is reduced in the world's eyes to the level of mere religion. This is more tragic than the false worship of a false god. What is mind-bending to me is that those who say they believe in God cloud what non-believers might be able to glimpse of the truth in God because of our fence-riding allegiances. We have one foot in the world and the other one supposedly in God's work, all while we spend the vast majority of our time trying to get an unregenerate society to support our way of thinking.

The Apostles lived and worked to spread the Gospel of the Kingdom through the competition of ideas. This means that the early church had to present that which could not be had in society, to bring about societal competition. They lived truth over and against living in, with and through an organized mandatory public cult (a cultural institution) such as the Romans or Jews employed. People saw the light of Christ and were drawn away from the world and its religions to the Truth, because the disciples lived openly towards society. They did not hide their candle under the basket of society's protocol. Neither did they make their teaching palatable, i.e. compromised, to where the world would welcome them into its public arena. We were meant to be cities set on a hill, separate from the world by exclusive truth but not separated from it by reclusive living.

Where Do We Start

The text in Philippians 3, being supported by many other scriptures, in addition to the practices of the church before Constantine, advocated respect for others in society, even if they held wrong opinions. This is the beginning behind the mindset of influence. Influence is a total contrast to manipulation and control, which are not in keeping with the concepts of Ambassadorship we covered in Chapter 14, *What Are We More Than Others*. Secondly, one cannot be an ambassador to his own people. We need to begin thinking as foreigners.

Some modern writers seem to understand the difference between domination and influence, even if not having exactly made the correlations of their teaching to church/state relations. One specific example is Dr. Larry Crabb in his book, *The Marriage Builder*. He articulates a super concept that is applicable to every relationship and relational issue known to man. The book is obviously about marriage, but there is no rule to say we shouldn't apply these concepts to every dealing between people or groups of people, such as in political/social constructs.

In the chapter entitled "Soul Oneness," under the subsection, "What Is Your Real Goal," Crabb propounds two foci we can have in regards to other people. They are "The Principle of Ministry," and "the Principle of Manipulation." Regarding ministry, Dr. Crabb emphasizes that ministry is meeting others' needs from a strong position of realizing who we are and that God is our source. Manipulation on the other hand has to do with focusing on our needs and wants and trying to jockey and jive others into meeting those needs by any means possible.[2] We are to be ministers of God to the world around us. We can't minister to people if we are trying to manipulate them to support our way of thinking.

Contrasting The Activist's Approach With Paul's

Many people today use their earthly citizenship as some sort of trump card or "right" with which to manipulate society in their favor. This is opposite of the biblical example. Paul took himself seriously when he said in Philippians 3 that everything he was before Christ was worthless in the way that it had been of value before. Look at the precursor to the book of Philippians in Acts 16:16-40. The story of Paul first coming to Philippi unfolds for us and we can see Paul indeed lived what he taught in the epistle to the Philippians. Paul got into a situation where charges were being whipped up against him and Silas. This resulted in the both of them being beaten with rods. Paul endured this treatment as a citizen of Rome according to the flesh but more importantly as a citizen of Heaven according to the Spirit.

The city of Philippi was a Roman colony populated by retired legionnaires and other Roman citizens looking for the opportunity provided by a "frontier" province. In the days following the altercation between the angry democratic mob and Paul, the city fathers started to expel Paul and Silas from their city and environs. At this point Paul drops the bombshell. He reveals that he too is a Roman citizen. The city leaders were shaking in their sandals for fear of their very lives, because they had abused a Roman citizen without trial or proper protocol. All of a sudden they became very conciliatory to Paul and Silas.

Can you read between the lines of Acts 16:38-40? *The chief magistrates gave Paul a key to the city and use of the local hall for services.* Of course, this is stretching it a bit. Paul did not leave Philippi immediately, but continued the Kingdom work there, before he moved on. But because Paul did not use his citizenship to save his skin, as would be humanly natural to do, the Kingdom enjoyed great success in that city. Specifically, because of how Paul handled playing his citizenship card, the work of the Kingdom was unparalleled. Paul must have been listening to God and acting under God's direction because it was unnatural to do as Paul did, and it was blessed in a miraculous way.

Many activists would seize upon this story and say, apparently Paul did value his earthly citizenship. This could be true; however it would be difficult to preach one thing and yet do another. Additionally, if his identity was really tied up in his earthly citizenship, using it would have been a first string of defense, as it is today. Paul realized that his citizenship in Rome meant nothing because of his new identity and purpose in Christ. He also realized that the world continued to recognize this distinction of citizenship in an earthly sense. Therefore, since they still viewed Paul from an earthly point of view, he could use this understanding as a tool for the purpose of God.

Disassociation

Paul did not use his earthly recognized citizenship as his first line of defense. Paul used his citizenship only three times in scripture, (*cf.* Acts 16:16-40, 22:23-30, 25:8-12). In each case, these were last-ditch efforts, where Paul had no other alternative, or where the gospel would be served in doing so. We can't know how much God specifically directed Paul on this point but in one case it is noted in scripture that God told him that he would go to Caesar, (*cf.* Acts 23:11). It is clear that Paul was cooperating with God.

There is further evidence of Paul's disassociation from the usual connections in the flesh. Paul draws a distinction between the Kingdom of God and the people of society, (*cf.* Gal. 6:10). In three cases Paul writes about our conduct towards "outsiders," (*cf.* I Cor. 5:12, Col. 4:5, and I Thes. 4:12). Paul makes another distancing comment in Romans 9:3 when he refers to the Jews as, "his kinsmen according to the flesh."

If Paul still saw himself as a Jew, why did he make this comment: "my kinsmen, according to the flesh"? It was because he was not thinking in fleshly concepts anymore.

The phrase "according to the flesh" occurs 17 times in the NT under Paul's hand, which indicates a strong message of disassociation from thinking in physical terms to thinking in spiritual realities. Paul was not alone as Peter, early in Acts, refers to the leaders of the Jews as "your rulers," suggesting this same disassociation, (*cf.* Acts 3:17). In I Peter 2:12, Peter exhorts his readers to, "Keep your behavior excellent among the Gentiles."

Why would Peter tell those who had been born Gentile to act right towards the Gentiles, unless he was speaking of a disassociation in mindset from physical to spiritual?

These texts and examples are in total contrast to the modern "Christian" activists who once again base their whole operation on a "worldly" recognized identity and an established institution within society. There is no distancing nor disassociative mindset for the religious conservative. They are comfortably sitting in the lap of society and definitely want to stay there. They operate from a standpoint of "rights" understood and granted by earthly systems rather than through

God's provision and direction for them. The contrast between the intent of scripture and the modern practices is so stark it is unbelievable that someone in recent years has not exposed these incongruities for what they are.

Whatever Happened To Prayer?

Is prayer something we do at the last minute when there is nothing else left to do?

Is prayer in the modern church the equivalent to inactivity?

One fellow has seen the tendency in the modern church on this point and wrote:

"One soon becomes aware of the idea that politics constitutes a sort of ultimate issue for the Christian. For some not to engage is a betrayal of the entire Christian life. Politics becomes a test of the sincerity of one's faith. The political order takes on such importance that all teaching seems to converge on this entrance into politics. Bible passages, which clearly have nothing to do with the question, are interpreted in a straight political sense. *One rejects (or forgets) those biblical passages which minimize politics, or which treat it as a sphere of activity which is evil.*" [3]

Is prayer seen by activists as sticking one's head in the sand?

Why is prayer not the first line of action in "our struggle" and way of living?

The modern churchgoer must not really believe the Bible on this aspect. If they did, we could see it explicitly called for in their published material and evident in the lifestyle of the church. As it stands, the actions of the average churchgoer are consistent with those who still identify themselves as American, who stand to lose by way of a liberal winner in politics. Is God's hand weakened by any person like a potential Hillary Clinton in the White House, or an Adolph Hitler, Mao Zedong or anyone else for that matter? Are God's hands tied by totalitarians, anarchy or any political system? Is God surprised when some liberal, socialist or despot comes to power? How we answer these questions may imply subtleties about what ideas we really live by.

The organized church reacting to various political situations in this country suggests that many believers act as though God were asleep and suddenly startled by the things that happen to us. The problem is not that God's hand is short but that we are so enmeshed in the world's thinking and ways of living that we have forgotten the truth and have accepted lies that darken our minds. We are not resting in truth but are being whipped back and forth by every wind of suspicion, intrigue and teaching. We have forgotten our work. We have forgotten our weapons of war. We have forgotten the example of Christ and the Apostles. We also have forgotten the example of the early church. If we did not think we have a stake in this country, we would be more concerned about what God is concerned about.

We need to repent and turn back to God, which is probably a different kind of prayer than most believers in this country would ever consider necessary. Yet, if this country is off track morally, believers need to take care of our own idolatry first before we call the world's society to repent. The modern church is not following God. So how can those around us, who don't know God, do what God wants? The text of II Chronicles 7:14 is an indictment against people who call themselves "my people," not just the common people of Israel. Paul said, "He is not a Jew (meaning a follower of God) who is one on the outside," (*cf.* Rom. 2:28-29).

The text in II Chronicles 7:14, which so many conservatives quote during times of reflection on where this country is going lists four things that we are to *apply* from this scripture.

1. Humble ourselves
2. Pray
3. Seek His face
4. Turn from *our* wicked ways (not the nations')

This scripture was given to Israel for a particular time of application; with a principle *that could* apply to believing people at other times in history. It is interesting to note that this scripture was given at a time of prosperity when Israel was dedicated to God, not a time of distress or moral decay. Additionally, the adage "heal our land" has to do with the ground [terra-firma], not a geo-political entity, as is commonly thought today. This verse suggests that believers are the ones in need of getting right with God, not a nation exclusively or inclusively. If we are going to evoke this text, we need to make sure we are not looking at God as some kind of cosmic Coke machine, from which we get what want if we push all the right spiritual buttons.

God's purpose may call for the destruction of a country or a system in His timing. He may not answer affirmatively every time to those who believe in Him, even those who also do the four things that are mentioned in the II Chronicles text. Remember if we ask anything *in His will or name,* He will do it. In a word, we would be asking for what Christ would ask. To do this we need to know the mind of God on a thing before we ask. God is not going to be shanghaied by our desires or requests. A lump of clay that is being molded does not ask the potter, "Why am I molded this way?" It is not our place to do so. We must be malleable to the Master's hand. Being moldable will not be convenient or comfortable from a human point of view. If we "the clay" are not workable in God's hand we are worthless for the purpose of our existence as followers of Christ.

Other Details About Prayer

We are instructed to pray for those in authority over us. This means that we are to pray for what God wants and for that which will bring peace and tranquility. We are to pray for God's leading, both for ourselves and for those in power. We are to be in prayer about the degenerative situations of society, to get God's mind and to implore Him to move for His name and reputation's sake. When we pray we ought to listen. Prayer is not barraging heaven with all sorts of concerns. Prayer is both asking and listening, i.e., communicating with God and He with us.

Prayer is trusting God with the outcome and not thinking we have to control it ourselves. Prayer is a form of resignation. But prayer is what we do first, not what we do after all other activities have failed. Hezekiah did not do all sort of political/military jiving when the Assyrian army was parked outside his door; he sought the Lord, (*cf.* II Kings 18:13~19:36).

Additional Considerations

What about the applications of texts commonly touted concerning submitting to governmental authority? Romans 13:1-7 and I Peter 2:13-15 are among those most commonly mentioned by church leaders.

Does submission mean absolute blind obedience or compliance?

Alternatively, does submission mean having a proper attitude towards government, while our actions may go against what this authority might require?

Putting it simply, can I respect an authority while at the same time disobeying it and still be righteous in God's sight?

On the precedent of Daniel and his friends in Babylon, I would say we could. In addition, we have the precedent of Peter and John before the Jewish rulers in the NT. Moreover, we also have Paul on his last trip to Jerusalem where he defended the gospel before Jewish leaders, before having to go in front of Felix, Festus, King Agrippa and ultimately Caesar.

We Need To Live According To What Is True.

1. We are citizens of Heaven and should act accordingly. This means that God is the sole motive and director of our activities. Our loyalties are to Heaven alone. We respect those around us and the law but we are not loyalty-bound to anything but God.

2. Because we are citizens of Heaven and servants of the Most-High God, we are to live to a higher standard. This means that if we are living out of His strength and provision, we will excel at everything that pertains to life and living on the earth because our motivation and provision to accomplish is both pure and endlessly being supplied by God.

3. We are to live in the world yet we do not march to its beat. We move along with the world for the purpose of being a light and witness yet we maintain a separateness. Some have interpreted this "separation" as looking different, e.g., appearance/clothes or living in physical separation, e.g. monks, communes, or the separatism of the pilgrims' ideas and practices. These ideas are man's interpretations of what they think they see in Christ and "godliness." It is in fact foolishness and does not reflect Christ or His teachings.

Paul was a citizen of Rome yet he did not use his rights as a citizen in the way the world used it. He honored the system without indulging in it for his own selfish reasons. Neither did he attempt to synchronize the world's thinking and motives into Christian living. As an example of this type of syncretism in modern situations, some religious leaders and well-known radio personalities today make voting equivalent to what is considered to be "Christian-living." To define voting as a "Christian" responsibility, is an absolute fabrication! (*cf.* Gal. 1:6-9) Where can anybody turn and show texts defining Christian responsibility as voting? Surely, one has to abrogate many other texts to use one text to support such an idea.

We have a responsibility to God and God alone in what we do! For some this will mean voting and for many others that will mean abstaining. All is dependant on what God is saying! Remember what Christ said? "I do nothing on My own initiative, but I speak these things as the Father taught Me," (*cf.* John 8:28, 12:49, and 14:10). Remember also that we are to be imitators of Him, (*cf.* I Cor. 11:1 and especially Eph. 5:1). Voting for the lesser of two evils just to perpetuate a system may not be God's bidding. Voting for what seems to be good based solely on issues based ideas, i.e. "voting pro-life," may not be consistent with listening to God and doing what He says. God may tell us to vote for a Pharaoh, meaning a totally ungodly person, because it suits His purpose, (*cf.* I Kings 19:14-17, Jer. 25:9). Nebuchadnezzar, Cyrus and even Caesar were God's servants. Would these guys have had your vote?

Paul as well as Peter and John displayed the attitude of honor for the rules of men in government while maintaining their God-given focus and directives. The Apostles did not ask the government if they could meet or preach. Nor did the apostles obey God's authority among men when the rulers said not to preach in Jesus' name. We are FREE to do anything that God has given us to do. This is by no means an approval to thumb our nose at any government. We should always try to work within the confines of what the government allows, but we are not to resign to it, allowing it to shape, direct, or define us. We are not to automatically default to the government's thinking and ways of doing things.

Jesus said the gates of hell will not prevail against "the church." What we've considered to be the "church" these days is being prevailed upon daily! This can only mean one thing: our concept of "church" is not really the church at all. If we continue to call the institution we've come to think of as "the church," then we are saying God is a liar. *The church* is not an institution that has been given a place in society by a governments of the world's system. God has given us a place and that is to be an alternative to society's religion and false worship. Whatever God shows us to do, no matter what the system of this world says, God will provide, and guide what He has directed us to do. If we want the systems of men to accept us and give us place we will never do the radical things God wants to do through His church in this country.

Paul existed in the world's system and did everything he could to continue his mission without coming into conflict with the civil authorities. This shows respect for the institutions of men while maintaining the independent objective of the Kingdom of God. Paul did everything in his means to avoid difficulty. Once he was lowered in a basket down the walls that fortified the city of Damascus to avoid a government-sponsored assassination, (*cf.* Acts 9:22-25). He even appealed to Caesar to avoid local problems, (*cf.* Acts 25:11, 28:19). He asserted his worldly citizenship in Philippi to advance the gospel in that city, (*cf.* Acts 16). He used his citizenship in ways to get around political groups seeking to misuse their power against him in his mission, (*cf.* Acts 22:23-30). He pitted two factious groups against each other to escape their agenda to get rid of him, (*cf.* Acts 23:1-12). He spoke to rulers as mere men, contending for the gospel of truth. Paul even used his captivity, and his transportation to that captivity, for the purposes of the Gospel. Paul NEVER diverted from this objective, (*cf.* Acts 27-28). He said "be imitators of me."

How could we in our modern era divert into all sorts of unsanctioned, unbiblical and divergent activities and still think we are following Jesus and the Apostles?

We need to be reconstituted in the truth and live out of the heritage that we have in Christ and His Kingdom rather than the heritage, identity and side-track we as believers in this country have bought into accepted teaching. Many over the years have asked me if I have a sense of debt to those over whose gun barrel my "freedom" was secured. My answer to that question is this, "Freedom is not cheap but what kind of freedom are we talking about? Spiritual Truth, which is the only true freedom, was bought and paid for by a greater host of people, including Christ Himself, down through the centuries than the freedom that is worshipped here in America. If we are truly followers of Christ, then we have a greater debt to Him and those who came before us in pursuit of spiritual truth and the freedom it brings, than we do to those who bought and paid for truth's pale cousin liberty."

I do enjoy the freedom that I have in this country; however, the warning that Paul gives us in regards to using freedom to sin comes to mind. We as the church have wasted our freedom and sinned through it by having exchanged service and loyalty to God for a simple mental assent about being committed. We have a very poor outflow of service and responsibility to the Kingdom as a result. This has all happened because our "freedom" has become our new god and the Lord of the Universe is put-off because we've been overcome by commitment to our newly found god. These are strong words, but seek the Lord and see what He says. It cannot be said enough, we need to hear from God or all that we do is mere building sand on top of sand.

18

Stratagem

Often success in military action is achieved largely by strategy. Strategy many times trumps wit, timing and in some cases even superior firepower. Certainly all these other aspects can help to make or break a conquest. But strategy is how you play the game once you have been dealt your hand in the altercation. We cannot do much about the situation of the culture around us in the way of using politics. The political solutions of the conservative right may be a major contributor to the culture being the way it is and the organized church being as insignificant to the culture as it has become. It is high time we take stock of who we are, as we discussed in Chapter 14, *What Are We More Than Others*. We have already discussed our objective as the church throughout this work. We have discussed that we are in a battle that rages from both within as well as all around us. We have some understanding of our enemy and his ability. But how do we use all that we know to both win the battle that is set before us and stay on the narrow road of what God has commanded us to do? It is this question with which we must struggle.

In this section, we will look at many verses to gain a better picture of how to live in the world while not being of it. We will see how to be wise as serpents but harmless as doves. As I was approaching this book it was apparent that an another entire book could be written on just scriptures alone which apply to church/state relations, especially drawing attention to those texts that are not applied in current applicative views today. It is the author's desire to invest a sizeable portion of scripture in this work. At the same time it is also the author's desire, while asking tough questions that need to be answered as well as reasserting scriptures that have been forgotten, not to dissect and explain so much that the reader is handed a completely prepared mental dinner. This would only facilitate the tendency of the modern church to cerebrally collect ideas on which they agree. In struggling with the material each of us can individually gain our own understanding and applications as God guides. Struggle will give us a better hold on what we discover. Thus we will be better prepared to employ truth rather than mentally collecting it.

Too many common views in the church today are supported by only small portions of pre-digested scripture. It is neither wise nor right to use scripture in this way when we have been given so much more that has applications to what we are doing in any area of ministry work. We have looked at many scriptures over the course of framing the issues of church/state relations and drawing attention to shortcomings in current applications. Now we need to focus on certain practical details that will allow us to live in the world while not forgetting our purpose as disciples. Again, it is the intent of this author to stir thought.

In discussing our strategy let me say that our enemy is not stupid. He is a master of distraction and disguise, changing appearances and approaches to confuse people. For years, thousands of years, the idea of citizenship and society had its basis in being compliant or suffering the cost. It was a coercive situation. Authority structures were rough and coarse, wielding power and abusing it. Under democracy, however, the enemy has attempted to trick people into thinking we as people have advanced and come out of the Dark Ages and Medieval times of "might makes right" thinking. The brutishness of the Dark Ages seems to have been replaced with the soft and welcoming entrance of "choice" and "tolerance" in democracy.

The old adage "honey will attract more flies than vinegar" is absolutely true. The devil used the old ways of governing to damn people just as he uses "new" ways do the same thing today. One existence made you grit your teeth to the grave. The other is currently rotting the moral fiber and anesthetizes any resistance people might have because there seems to be no evil to resist. And so we drift off into total inactivity on the real war front because all seems well in the physical world on which we've mistakenly concentrated. People will willingly trade oppression and heavy handedness for "choices" and soft living any day. However, either can be bad and just as damning if we do not realize what is truly happening and walk in God's provision and direction.

Over the years, it has become apparent to me that strategy is perceived by some to be underhanded. Strategy seems to have a connotation akin to conspiracy. Yet, strategy is the very key to getting anything done in life. It involves a central plan to accomplish an objective in the face of obstacles. Without a plan, life and work are impossible, at least as far as being accomplished and successful. Strategy is related to the Integrated-Thinker we addressed in Chapter 7, *Mis-Identity As A Motivator For Political Activism.*

The absence of strategy in the church, pertaining to contending with the world and accomplishing our objective despite the obstacles the world presents, is evident by the tendency of the organized church towards either *separatism/isolationism* or *coercion/ domination.* These are the chief techniques used by religious people to remain "pure" and unspotted by the evil world. In separatism we turn away from being as Jesus was, being in the world but not of it, to being in the world but separate from it. Separatism is a concept the Puritans employed. Equally, in coerciveness we also turn away from being like Jesus (in the world but not of it) to being in the world by rejoining its game to become the most dominant player. Since separatism didn't work for the Puritans, neo-Puritans (the conservative right) have turned to the coercive/ dominating approach. People with the mindset of domination get right down in the hog trough of the world, because they believe that their separateness is in their belief system alone.

In the above paragraph we can see the opposite ends of the spectrum lived out within what is called "the church." No doubt, the opposite ends of the philosophical spectrum grow from tiny specks of truth that take on a life of their own. If you question their adherents, sifting through the opposite ends of their extremes you will find the essence of truths that have been taken to illogical extremes. We as disciples should be able to respond to any situation by looking at the many Bible examples God in His infinite wisdom has provided for us to use. But if we take one approach, moralizing it to an absolute, we make ourselves imbalanced and less useful to God. The balance is to be in the world while not being of it. This seems to have been a tough balance for the church to strike. If we take another look at Christ and what He said, we will see a few points which will help clear up the problems and misunderstandings about this delicate balance between politics/society and the church.

Christ revealed early on in His work with the disciples that standing for Him was going to be difficult from the human perspective. He hinted at persecution as early as Matthew 5:10, and then directly in Matthew 10. Christ did not mean us to be gluttons for punishment, willy-nilly throwing ourselves to martyrdom. Each of us has been given a purpose and role to play with the expectation of fulfilling that role and responsibility. The world, the flesh and the devil stand in the way of these God given objectives, which thus puts us in a battle as we press on to accomplish what God has ordained. We get into a whole peck of trouble as well as become worthless to God if we choose to pursue the distractions the enemy provides. This is a paramount issue, we must not to be led astray. Paul many times warned about being lead astray, so we ought to be aware.

The major key for us is knowing God's word, learning to know God's voice and listening to be obedient. It is simple yet it is difficult. It is easy because God has provided everything we need to be successful in His employ. In actuality He has won in the absolute sense and so our work should be just a cooperation with His direction. This is difficult because our flesh and the world press us back towards responding to their stimuli out of our "old man" rather than the way God would direct. We should resist the world and its ways because they are a trap. We should resist the mindless application of systematic thought because it subverts operating out of relationship with God. Systemology is a quick way to miss God.

Jesus made the statement, "Be shrewd as serpents, and innocent as doves," in Matthew 10:17b. This verse holds a key to the balance between spiritual isolationism, as practiced by the Puritans or the monastics, and the excesses of *sacralism** in the form

---

*Footnote:** The word "sacral" is defined back on page 152

adopted by modern religious conservatism holding to the Constantinian change. The balance is maintained by focusing on our objective and surrendering to the Holy Spirit's creativity to go around the obstacles of the world in order to accomplish God's will.

As you read texts in the Bible on the subject of our relationship to the world you will find that Jesus, Paul, Peter and James used various strategies when living out the objectives of a disciple's life. While God is not limited to these examples they are an excellent place to start. The following is just a small list of details to keep in mind regarding our responses and exchange with the world. Implicit in the ideas of this book is the conclusion that the church will experience more and more aggressive behavior from the world's society as we get closer to doing what we should about our responsibilities as disciples. This increase in world-generated adversity is a clue that we are getting "warmer," i.e., closer to the truth.

Know Whose Backyard You're "Playing" In

It is important to know that we, as disciples, are automatically in an adverse environment. This world is the devil's. This point is very clear in scripture. Certainly God is sovereign; however, a limited license has been given the enemy. This fact is clearly referred to in the accounts of Jesus' temptation in the desert, (cf. Matt. 4:8-11, Luke 4:6). Christ did not deny Satan's claim. In the book of Job it is said that the devil wanders about on the earth, which indicates that he has dominion and power to do so. I Peter 5:8 warns us that the devil prowls around like a lion seeking to devour the unwary. This also depicts the devil's dominion on the earth. Jesus refers to the devil as the "ruler of this world" three times in the Gospel of John, (cf. John 12:31, 14:30, and 16:11). This is not meant to scare us as disciples but to make us aware. The Bible tells us to be sober and alert.

If you were to knowingly enter a yard where a vicious dog is known to be lurking about, you should be careful of life and limb. You should have respect for a certain set of teeth that could do great damage to your posterior. We need to know our place in the world and who it is that is running this world, albeit in a limited sense. The problem believers have had since the Constantinian change is that they have thought that we, as the church, are the foundation of modern society (establishment mentality). This is at best only half true. The world has borrowed the church's truths of discipline, character, ways of governing, and various other activities. But they have reengineered these truths to work on a purely human level where they will be acceptable to the irreligious as well as the devout. There is no room for exclusivity in wide public appeals and so God is shoved out of the equation in this process of syncretism. The problem is, that what's left is something that has a form of godliness but at the same time denies the power of God, (cf. II Tim. 3:5).

It is very important that we know where we are and that we live according to that understanding. Give respect and honor to whom it is due. Be on alert for the tricks of the devil in deception and alluring presentations. Remember the forbidden fruit and how attractively the enemy presented it.

Don't Let Our Objectives And Focus Be Divided

Jesus was accused of using the devil to cast out the devil, (cf. Luke 11:15-23). Jesus' response was remarkable and a principle was articulated. Division is the first step to destruction. Before destruction occurs, incapability sets in as a result of the divisions. If the enemy can divide our unity, purpose, relationship, or identity we become ineffective and weak. Paul warns Timothy to KEEP what has been entrusted to him and not to get involved with discussions of "so-called" knowledge that only lead to arguments about nothing. In other words, focus on God's objectives and do not be divided from it, (*cf.* I Tim. 6:20).

In John 17 Jesus prayed for unity of purpose and fellowship. Fellowship and unity are primary to our objective. If our supply lines are cut-off, i.e., fellowship and unity, our effectiveness will also be cut down. The Bible speaks plainly against being double-minded which means having split affinities. Jesus spoke of it in Luke 16:13 and the Apostle James also spoke out in James 1:4-8, 4:8. It is clear that anyone, no matter how extraordinary their capability, will be negatively affected by going in two directions at the same time. Yet this is what the modern church in America advocates! It lives as the world does, whoring after all the objects of lust the world runs after, while mentally thinking it is pure and chaste pursuing God. What nonsense! Without focus, discipline and a sense of reality we will be useless to God, (*cf.* I Cor. 9:25).

Be Shrewd, (cf. Matt. 10:16, I Cor. 4:5)

Being shrewd sometimes conjures up negative ideas for people. Yet being shrewd really just means being wise. We should be wise not only to our craft and objective, but also to the resistance factors and perpetrators of divisiveness. Knowing whose backyard you're playing in is a part of being wise; however, we need to be more specific and detailed.

1. Silence and not revealing all we know, (*cf.* Josh. 2:1-15, Acts 16).

2. Knowing when to speak and when not to, (*cf.* Matt. 10:17-20, Mark 14:59-61a, John 18:33-38 to John 19:8-10, Acts 16:19-24 and Acts 22:23-30).

3. Necessary Compliance, (*cf.* Matt. 17:24-27,

22:15-21, Rom. 13:7, Titus 3:1-2, I Pet. 2:17).

4. Use the factious nature of politics and national-ism for our own purposes, (*cf.* Acts 13:43-46, 22:23-30, 23:6-10).

5. Fleeing known opposition when it comes to end-ing life or ability to continue ministry if possible, (*cf.* Matt. 10:23, 12:14-16, Luke 4:28-31, Acts. 9:22-25, 13:50-51, 14:4-7, 23:14-31).

6. Avoiding confrontations with the world other than for the Gospel, (*cf.* Matt. 17:24-27, Acts 4:19-20, 5:28-35).

There are many details to being "shrewd" in our dealings with the world. If we are being persecuted, we should take measures to do our work incognito so that we can continue and be as safe as possible without becoming inactive. We don't stop; we find "creative ways" to do what we are supposed to do. If we live in a free society, we don't sit down in it and relax. A free society is no better an option for the disciple than a society that is closed with a forced belief. The world is made up of only two kinds of people, believers and non-believers. Therefore, a free society is just as bad to settle down into as an oppressive one would be for the believer. We are in a war, whether an active war or a "cold war," we are still in a battle. We cannot be joined to anyone other than Christ and His Kingdom, the church, which must not be diluted.

Never Settle Back Into Civilian Living, (cf. II Tim. 2:3-4)

On the heels of the last section, we cannot become a civilian in this world spiritually or physically speaking. James 4:4 states, "You adulteresses, do you not know that friendship with the world is hostility toward God? Therefore whoever wishes to be a friend of the world makes himself an enemy of God." Romans 12:2 says, "Do not be conformed to this world but be transformed by the renewing of your mind." When we come to Christ we are transformed to another status and we are not to go "back to Egypt." Having said this we are to continue to choose to follow and cooperate with Christ. Our walk is a process not a "beam me up, Scotty" transfer from one life into another.

The word "soldier" is used figuratively in the NT at least six times. The term has literal meaning as well. Struck by the emphasis on this terminology in the NT General William Booth, founder of the Salvation Army, regimented his organization in the form of a literal army of enlistees, officers, ranking and so on. For years their effect evangelistically was immense. The "soldier" imagery of the NT is an effectual way of depicting the living out of separation and call to duty that God wants us to live, but this does not mean isolationism. Too many times in church history separation has been interpreted in the ways of isolation. Soldiering does not in any way allow for this easy way out of separation combined with duty.

Too many believers have correlated the separation the Bible speaks of to mean what we could call "compound-christianity." This is where people hole-up in a "separate" place to stay out of circulation in the world. As soldiers of Christ, this cannot be true for us. We are in an active battle with the spirit behind this world that is trying to take prisoner as much of mankind as he can. We cannot get away somewhere and still be involved with setting captives free. If I were in the Army, I would still be part of this country, yet I would set aside for the purpose of defense or offense on behalf of the country. We have a purpose, reason and objective, which are beyond the mere physical world of the unbeliever.

Respect The Authority Of The World's Political Structures (cf. Rom. 13:1-7)

This is where we get into deep water. People have various opinions as to what this text in Romans means. Many believe that in order to "respect" we need to do everything the world system of power throws at us. This is absolutely false! Paul says beware lest we be distracted from the purposes given to us by God. Peter and James supported this view by their actions, (cf. Acts 4:19, 5:28-35).

God established government as a means of order in a fallen world. The world is fallen and so there is no expectation on the part of God, nor should there be on ours, that the governments of this world will be just, fair, good, or anything else other than a form of order that God has made. God's laws are perfect but there is also such a thing as free will. Man or governments made up of men can either abide by God's designs or not. God will certainly judge wrong behavior and encourage or bless the right. However, man in his fallen state abiding by God's laws is not what God ultimately wants. God wants people to love Him by admitting who He is and then choosing to obey Him for Him alone.

God has appointed earthly rulers in either an active or passive sense. And we, as ambassadors of His Kingdom, are to respect and honor those of other kingdoms. It is that stark! We are of another kingdom that is not made of hands nor marked by boundaries. We recognize the world forms and structures and participate in them only as we have to or as we are instructed to by God. If what we were before Christ is dead to us because we have been raised in newness of life, how can we do any differently?

There is real spiritual war needing to be done within the church on this area alone. There are generational ruts and territorial issues which need to be torn down on the issue of our identity in a complete sense as it plays out to the world around us. There are 1600+ years of tradition to unravel. Evangelicals condemn certain parts of the historical church because of its tendencies towards the worship of tradition, yet they themselves worship the same kinds of tradition wrapped in different paper.

Reconsider: Respect for Authority Structures

A. Not to be limited in ministry because of being committed to trying to manipulate the world's systems of government.

If we have a specific job or focus in the Kingdom we can't be effective if we are multi-tasking and dividing our energies and attention among several areas of focus. There is the need of doing various functions in our lives, but when over-commitment happens, this is where we get into trouble. Since we only have one "founding father"* there are no others to which to be dedicated. We can work in infiltrating operations in the world's system, but we do not need to see any of their founding fathers as ours. In addition, not everybody should be recruited for these types of special operations, because they are a tough balance. In real life if people were indiscriminately put into covert military operations, standards would suffer and keeping stealth would be impossible. Those who are recruited for this kind of service are taught and trained to cover their covert activities with public work so as to maintain covert viability. Maintaining the viability of the undercover operation is always the goal. This kind of occupation is not for everybody. God specifically selected, implanted and guided a very small number of His servants down through biblical history to mix with

*Footnote: This is in direct opposition to those who claim the "founding fathers" of this country as theirs, or who would associate importance of these "founding fathers" to who or what we are as followers of Christ.

the world systems of their day to accomplish His purpose. Look at David, Samuel, Daniel, Moses or any of the Judges, to name a few.

Secondly, look at Bible the record regarding people who respected the world's authority structures yet disobeyed them. We can see that God can place us in situations where we are not trying to gain power and use it to force compliance to God's will, such as religious conservatives advocate today. Yet, we can lead and make very powerful statements for God and His purposes through the direct work to which God calls us. God though, must be the one putting us in these places, or it will be no different than the top-down cultural conquests of the Conservative Right, (*cf.* Exod. 1:15-19, 2:2-4, Josh. 2:1-6, Dan. 3: 4-21, 6:1-17, Matt. 2:1-12, Acts 4:19-20, 5:28-35).

B. Use of worldly understood status and systems in ways which do not limit our ability to accomplish our purposes.

The world goes about its business with no understanding or care for the follower of Christ and what changes have taken place as a result of conversion. Because of this, we still have a credible audience with the world through our former identities and relationships with them. These are currencies they understand. Because they still see us the way we were, we can use what they still think of us for God's purposes. No longer are we citizens of earth for the purposes of whatever country we were from. Suddenly, we are citizens of heaven with another kind of dedication and loyalty. When the purposes of heaven are stalled by the systems of the world, *WE CAN* use the systems of the world to our advantage and purpose. (*cf.* Acts 16:16-40, 22:23-30, 23:5-10, 25:9-12). In each one of these texts, Paul used objects that the world understood and recognized for the purposes of God. His focus, dedication, loyalty, and purposes were all for heaven, not for his own selfish agenda or even to save his own neck. The Apostle's approach on this point is that the status the world still recognizes is a tool towards an end, not an end in itself as it has become in modern Evangelicalism.

Responding In An Opposite Spirit (cf. Matt. 5:44, Luke 6:28, Rom. 12:17)

This could be listed under being shrewd but I think it has its own specific character needing emphasis. We are naturally to respond in an opposite spirit instead of only taking up this mindset as defense or approach to a specific problem. The world is fairly animalistic, especially because of the worldview evolution has fostered, e.g., survival of the fittest. This is in exact diametric opposition to what Christ taught, i.e., vulnerability and meekness. Yet, if we seek to work through the political system the way it is established and the way that the world goes about its business we have to take on this animalistic mantra of domination and survival at any cost.

The verses cited above in this section assume that Christians generally will not have the dominant role in society. Christ spent much time preparing his disciples for the deluge of hate and mistreatment they would receive because they were following Him. It is also intimated that this persecution would take place because the disciples weren't to be a dominant part of society. Christ said the world will know us by our love, not by our attempt at cultural domination or political savvy, which are the only traits by which most conservatives are known. This inversion is tremendously sad. The world needs to see something different than itself when it looks at the follower of Christ. When we pursue political power, as has been done for the last 40-years, the world will not see Christ or His truth in us. We must take a more respectful, humble role by allowing God to place us where He will, as He did with all great leaders in the OT.

Do Not Voice Beliefs, Live Them Out (cf. Matt. 5:16, I Pet. 2:11-12)

What we believe will be demonstrated more by what we do than what we say. A class of missionaries in training was asked what they noticed about a teacher entering the room and walking through the class. Most had nothing to say but one mentioned the fragrance of perfume that the teacher was wearing. The teacher went on to say that most of the students would be going to places where they may not be able to communicate in words. What these students knew may be communicated through the fragrance of how they live. This way of communicating will be detectable to anyone.

It is so easy to politicize what we say we believe, and to make some sort of platform to stand on. Jesus never mentioned that He believed anything; He merely practiced what was true. He did not dialog about healing; He healed and made more of a statement than any well-executed debate ever could have. We have more to say to the world if we feed the poor, clothe the naked, teach the ignorant and proclaimed the truth of life to people that will make them new creations being directed by God, instead of trying to make laws in an attempt to corral people into mere moralistic behavior.

People were drawn to Christ; however, dogmatic and politically charged words only polarize and repel people. We need to get beyond this mindset that the world has dropped in our laps and begin to live out what Christ has taught us. This is the only way that the world will be drawn to God.

Don't Draw Attention To Ourselves In The Ways Of The World, (cf. I Thes. 4:11-12, Matt. 6:2-5, Phil. 3:2-6)

Jesus was careful not to draw attention to Himself to achieve His work, (*cf.* Matt. 4:5-7). Jesus did not seek the position of authority in men's thinking because God had given Him His place. As we do what God has shown us to do, God will give us place in this world to accomplish His plans. We have goals and objectives outside the world's ways of looking at life. Why turn aside to the Vanity Fair of life just because it has extended an invitation to join in, e.g., democracy. Politics, and all the other devices of men, seeks to draw attention to ourselves. If we do what God has ordained us to do, Christ will be lifted up and will draw all men unto Himself through our work.

Everything we were in the world means nothing in the Kingdom of God. Why try to make these points of focus the chief means of operation for the Kingdom of God? If we build a "house" in our own strength we are only building a monument to our foolishness, "Unless the LORD builds the house, They labor in vain who build it," (*cf.* Ps. 127:1).

Don't Wage War According To The Flesh, (cf. Matt. 26:49-55)

We're not to wage war according to the flesh. Our war in not a war of flesh but a spiritual war. Politics is very much a flesh and blood, physical world battle. If we wage war on the physical level we fail at the real battle. What is most true of any person, forgiven or unforgiven, is that they are a soul. There are only two kinds of souls in this world, those that are either being saved or those who need to begin this process.

We need to understand that, while we may be directed to do a work in the physical world through a capacity that the world understands, there is a much larger war being waged beyond what any of us could do through the physical realm. To admit that the bulk of our war goes on at a spiritual level is not to advocate becoming a recluse or spiritual weirdo. Yet, if we step into another man's game defined by that man's rules, we are stepping out of what God has for us, and we'll most certainly lose. Daniel never compromised what he was, nor did he seek after what the world's power structures offered to him as a means of effecting change. God put Daniel where He wanted him. God can put any of us in any position of authority in this world's system for His purpose. Be sure that He is putting you in places of power and that you are not seeking it for your own glory, even for a good purpose. Be very reluctant to be mainstreamed into the world's game.

Don't Be Defined Nor Subjugated By Political Language And Terms, (cf. Luke 5:19-24, John 8:3-9, Acts 23:6)

The law of politics is to identify one's opponent and either conquer or buddy up to him in order to achieve one's own objectives. Christ's way went between the extremes of the opposite sides on issues by either asking other questions that would take the discussion in a different direction or simply refusing to play a hand that others tried to deal to Him. Paul, on the other hand, used language that he knew would set two groups of his opponents against each other. We cannot let the world define us nor render us useless by joining either side in their arguments. We have our own gig and it may go along with something the world is doing, then again it may not. Our job is not to fit into the world's system, thereby being "of the world," but to tend to our job while we are yet in the world. We cannot do this job if we are responding or reacting to all the red herrings they send past us by way of issues, problems, crises or even challenges to our way of thinking. To respond to them in purely physical terms is to wage war according to the flesh.

We must press into God and allow Him to direct our paths. We cannot allow hollow religious ideas, nor the world's ulteriorly motivated sideshows, to pull us into the type of activity which turns out to upstage the main event—being the Kingdom of God amongst the kingdoms of men—for which we have been laid hold of by Christ. We must forget what lies behind and press forward in the upward call of Christ.

Postscript:

During the course of this book we've looked at the church's over-involvements in politics of trying to turn the tide in the culture wars in an attempt and bring America back from its moral freefall. While these objectives seem good in one sense, we have to weigh this "good" with the cost to the Kingdom of God as a whole. How has this focus supplanted the efforts toward what we as the church have been commanded to do? Since we live in an affluent culture, and most of us have money and time, what responsibility do we have to the Kingdom of God internationally when other places have less witness, money or means, to bring witness to their part of the world?

Proverbs 18:17 tells us, "The first to plead his case seems just, until another comes and examines." All seems good with the religious conservative mindset. But if we begin to look at all that is evident about these involvements, does it still warrant a full head of steam in that direction? For decades the Conservative Right has plied its case to the church in this country. The conservative view has gone virtually unchallenged as to the question of validity. Through this book we've considered many questions trying to frame the issue in ways that an entangled follower of Christ might be able to see what they may not have seen before. It is not my intent to berate anyone or to call into question anyone's integrity through this book.

Balance is a definite objective here, not absten-
tion. As mentioned before, mankind is funny in the
respect that if one objects to another's point of view in
any way the first thinks the second is totally opposite
and then engages them from this mindset. While there
is definite purpose and merit to working in politics
under God's direction, there is equally merit in other
works that God would have people do as well. The
point is that good arguments for some cause, or even
the severity of a seeming need, are not the determining
factors for why anyone should do anything about a
situation. There is no more or less desirable involvement in God's eyes than what He has told us to do. The
point is, to whom are we listening?

In all the presentations concerning political
action I have ever heard, there is a fevered push to
address a problem. I do not hear language that encourages believers to seek the Lord about what He would
have us do. It is always; "you must act now," or "we
have no time to lose" and the famous, "you can't stay
silent on this one." We are always caught reacting to
the flavor of the week in political/cultural meltdowns.
This is one of the details that got me thinking about
what is really going on with political action in the
church. This reactionary tendency is in stark contrast
to the Bible record. There is a plethora of scripture con-
trasting the modern ideas with the biblical examples,
(*cf.* II Kings 18, II Chron. 32, and Isa. 36-37).

The tendency of the church, historically speaking, has either been to be "out of the world," therefore
never running the risk of "being of the world," or it has
been too much into the world's ways of doing business
that it becomes indistinguishable from the world. Roland Bainton put it this way, "If there is no accommodation [to the culture] Christianity is unintelligible and
cannot be spread; if there is too much accommodation
it will be spread, but will no longer be Christianity."[1]

This volume is really all about focus, relationship and deaths. Focus because if we do not know who we are or where we are going we will probably never arrive at the destination we'd hoped for (to bring glory to God). The purpose of anything we do in ministry is to bring glory to God. What would bring more glory to God, you might ask, than a society living by God's law? The Bible tells us that God is not interested in societies that obey God's law in some formalistic duty. He desires people who would call Him "their God" and who love Him, "from every tribe people and nation."

The second aspect mentioned: relationship. This refers to our relationship to the world and to God. This may sound trite but the church, historically speaking, has not related to the world in the way we should because we have misunderstood our identity. In coming to God, Lordship is to have an effect on every area of our lives. Unfortunately, in the institutional church, Lordship is only taught on a couple of superficial levels. One of those levels is mental assent. Lordship teaching has either failed to touch identity issues or we have kept it from doing so by accepting mental assent as a legitimate form of conversion. The failure here is that we live under assumed identities with assumed motives—both of which have kept the Kingdom within this country from being truly effectual.

The third aspect mentioned: deaths! While many understand death to self, many more have not realized that "maturity in Christ calls for many more deaths. Death to Family," (cf. Luke 14:26) "Death to Country," (cf. Phil. 3:2-10, 3:20, Heb. 13:14) "and Death to Humanity,"[2] (cf. Luke 14:27, I John 2:6, I Cor. 4:13b). This type of teaching obviously is tremendously unpopular because it requires more than the "accepting Jesus" on a mental level. Without these other deaths we cannot walk with God, because we are not yet fully dead to our former trespasses and ways of thinking.

Effort has been made herein to provide as much scripture on the topic of church/state relationship as possible. Most common views about this subject today only use about 10% of the scripture that speaks to this subject. If we return to the scriptures and do what they really say, we will in effect accomplish the intent of all the political meddling of conservatives. Conversely, the involvements of the political conservative will by no means accomplish what God has clearly set out in scripture for the follower of Christ to do. The major difference is that we as followers of Christ will have to realize our true identity and begin to actually work at evangelism and discipling. This work *IS NOT* for a chosen few, but for everybody in the church. We cannot stage a platform of ideals and promote, promote, promote. The gospel of Christ is much more radical than a mere belief system or a political platform.

We need to get back to the basic gospel, the simplicity that Paul refers to in II Corinthians 11:3. If Christ died for the sin of all mankind in order that all men might bow before Him in personal surrender, ought we not to spend our time so that as many as would listen would also have the chance to hear? We can only be in one place at a time. If we are defending the "Judeo-Christian Ethic" we can't be sharing with those who've never heard the gospel in the first place. Romans 10:13-15 tells us:

> "for "WHOEVER WILL CALL UPON THE NAME OF THE LORD WILL BE SAVED." How then shall they call upon Him in whom they have not believed? And how shall they believe in Him whom they have not heard? And *how shall they hear without a preacher?* And how shall they preach unless they are sent? Just as it is written, "HOW BEAUTIFUL ARE THE FEET OF THOSE WHO BRING GLAD TIDINGS OF GOOD THINGS!"

The idea of reversing a culture's shift towards immorality sounds good. Yet when we begin to dissect the whole philosophy behind the how(s) and why(s) it becomes tawdry and self-serving. Let's begin to live the truth rather than submitting to the world's idea of religion as something to which we merely give mental assent. Let's truly die to *Self, Family, Country* and *Humanity* and follow Christ. Let's stop trying to give ourselves what we don't deserve in a place to call our own and see that our belonging is in the Kingdom of God. Let's stop allowing the world to shape our thinking and begin to impact it by living out Christ in their realms. One writer put is this way, "The Christian, in the New Testament sense of that word, is a sojourner. But to play well the part of a sojourner is no easy task. For a sojourner stands halfway between a native and a migrant; he must walk the thin line that separates total engagement [of the society around him] from total disengagement."[3]

We can live in the world and yet be separate from it in purpose by the way we do what God tells us to do. The world is not in need of another example of what it does by itself already. It is in need of those men and women who will follow Christ's footsteps and do only the things that Christ Himself did, but also the thing that He and the Father are doing today. God is not some ancient clockmaker who wound up the universe and let it run its course since the Bible was completed. He is still intimately involved with events and times in which we live. Isn't it time we allowed God to direct how we live and respond to the world around us rather than using narrow-minded, self-determined principles to guide how we protect our interests while we claim to be "serving God?" My hope is that we will be challenged about our thoughts and ideals relating to the church/state relationship and that we will seek God's heart on what we should do in our lives today.

COURAGE
IS NOT THE HAVING
OF A BELIEF
OR MOTIVATION,
BUT RATHER, IT IS THE
CHARACTER NECESSARY
TO CARRY THEM
BOTH OUT.

– Timothy L Price –

Scriptural Index

The scriptural texts listed here consist of every mentioned text in the course of this book. Some of the references stem from what others have quoted and/or twisted. However, the vast majority of the texts are in support of what we are talking about within the subject of church state relations and the believers true identity and heritage. All that the Bible has to say on this subject is not mentioned in this book. At the end of this section is direction on how to get more material.

I can provide you with further biblical resources on the topic of the church/state issue and the believers identity. There is not space or suitable means within this book to showcase all that the Bible has to say.

Go to:

www.kingdomcitizenship.org
"Resources Page" and look for the "scriptures" link.

Listing Of Influential Books And Materials

Part of the reason for this section is to give you the opportunity to gain a better understanding of some of the background that has opened my mind. Often when I read a book I would like to have known what was behind a writers' mindset besides what he quoted. Here is a chance for you to see some of the goodies that brought about the compilation of this work. I will list the sources and maybe some reasons why they are significant. There is no order in how they are listed or to what degree they have influenced me.

Spiritual Warfare, By Dean Sherman — This is the most balanced book concerning this subject I have ever read. It helped me to see that the fight is both in the world as well as inside our head, in the church as well as the way we were raised culturally. Most people who cover this subject only point to the world and exterior sources for the war we fight. This book brings a lot more into focus for us to consider.

Ten Shekels And A Shirt, By Paris Reidhead — (*Audio tape or digital sound recording*) This work is epic in its implications. First given in 1966, this message is still prophetic. Even today people have not begun to take apart all that this man said. We fail to realize how much of the world's thinking has crept into church living. This sermon shows how many ideals of the world have laid waste not only the liberal wing of the institutional church but also the Evangelical/ Fundamental and even Charismatic parts of the organized church. Reidhead's teaching can be compared to statistical studies and history since the recording to see the prophetic nature of this message.

The Open Church, By James Rutz — This work gives a very succinct view of how the Roman Emperor Constantine changed the church forever. It helps us to understand some of what we lost in the transition, between the Pre-Nicene church and Constantine's reinvention of the church, giving us hope as we look at retaking our stand as the church today.

Hearing God, By Peter Lord — This book has opened my mind to something that few dare to speak about today. The book is not only profound but also profoundly simple. In learning to listen to God we can live out of what He says to us today. Instead of being left to try and apply what God has said in the past that might relate to our situations today, reacting in our own strength, we can allow God to tell us what to do in concert with what He is already doing. We won't be fighting the hand of God nor will we be facilitating the enemy's agenda through our own well intended but fleshly efforts. We will be acting out of what God is saying. "Faith comes by hearing the word of God."

Blinded By Might, By Cal Thomas & Ed Dobson — For 5 to 7 years I was afraid to launch on my own book, *The Diluted Church*, even though I had done much of the research and was aware that it was needing to be done. Thomas' and Dobson's book got me started again. This is a good book that will give added perspective to the discussion of the church./ state relationship. I did not feel this book went far enough nor did it give much in the way of what we should do, hence the reason for my book. However, Cal & Ed showed great fortitude in standing up against some ideas they themselves had promoted which they now felt were incorrect.

The Second Coming Of The Church, By George Barna — George is a man after my own heart. Barna studies statistical information looking for trends and data that should help us make better choices and show us the error of our good intentions. Some leaders criticize his work because it has many negative implications. But we should not be afraid to see the truth. I quoted this book a fair amount because it is well worth the read.

The Reformers And Their Stepchildren, By Leonard Verduin — This book is excellent in that it gives the perspective of other people who lived and died by the ideas of stepping back from exclusively using the government as a stage for the church to do it work and step back into kingdom living. I find it encouraging to have come to the same conclusions others did without having exposure to them before I had my own understanding. It is in the best way confirming. This book will open the doors of history many everyday church people unfortunately know nothing about. It will give a very different perspective on what the church's relationship to the state should be.

Pilgrim Church, By E. H. Broadbent — This is a wonderful book of church history that helps us to understand where our heritage as followers of Christ really came from. It is not as well organized as Verduin's "Reformers" book, but it is an excellent work to educate us on where our allegiances should be due to our heritage as members of the Church internationally: the Kingdom of God.

The Unseen Hand, By A. Ralph Epperson — This work is good for giving us perspective on modern history. If we only read High School "history" or "providential history" we might get another view. This book helps us to understand that not all that we know about history is true and that any view is just as revisionistic as any other.

I do not agree with the author as far as that we can make a real change in the course of this world through the means of political interventions. Neither do I believe in conspiracy on the human level as this book tends to ply its case. However, the book is well documented and a worthwhile read.

Count Zinzendorf, By Felix Bovet — This is a wonderful biography of one of the most remarkable missionary thinkers of the modern church. This fellow lived in between organized "religion" and the state. He lived a precarious life of living relationship to the Lord rather than reacting to the state or the issue of the moment. The Moravians show us a wonderful picture of people whose affect we are still the benefactor of, who did not use the world's system of politics as a means to changing culture. Culture was changed as a by-product of their work, not the prime motive of their work.

Tortured For Christ, By Richard Wurmbrand — Another biography about a fellow who lived between organized religion and an oppressive state. This work is a breath of fresh air to the stale ideas of domination and procrustean techniques of cultural interventions through politics. Combined with his work: *From Suffering to Triumph*, Richard shows us that the world will come to us when we play our game God's way.

From Suffering To Triumph, By Richard Wurmbrand — This book read as an immediate addendum to *Tortured for Christ* helps one to see the truly extreme side of not taking political sides in ministry or life. Richard was able to preach and minister to those in the state who had been the source of the conflicts in his life. Because those in the oppressive state could not squelch him and could see that he was an alternative to extremism not the other half of an issue, God used him to bridge the gap between oppressor and the vengeful oppressed. This book is a testament to God's ways in modern times.

Alone With Christ, By Richard Wurmbrand — This book gives some insight into what God showed Wurmbrand about who he really was as a believer. This will give us much in the way of perspective as we are faced with divesting of the ideas of the conservative activist and reassert our true identity as the Kingdom of God amongst the kingdoms of men. It will help us see ourselves properly so that we can set about our work as Ambassadors.

Unveiled At Last, By Bob Sjogren — This is a wonderful book that paints a vivid pictures of idea that we are responsible to our kingdom. This is uncommon teaching today. There is responsibility that belongs to "the being" of what it means to follow Christ. Bob tells us that we are blessed, "top line" to be and make a "bottom line" blessing on the world around us. There is responsibility to pass on what we have been given both materially and spiritually. Many church people give passing agreement to this type of teaching but the facts of living it are next to nil. The author confronts this problem head-on.

One Shall Chase A Thousand, By Mable Francis — This biography tells about the life of a woman who was sold out to Christ, not country and not denomination. It shows the impact of her life on the country of Japan. It is encouraging to see a person give up what is normal for people (belonging and rights) so as not to play a part of this world's kingdoms and futile thinking. Mabel's impact on Japan was significant and this was directly tied to her approach and sacrifice. This woman was cut from the same cloth at Paris Reidhead.

The Early Christians, By Eberhard Arnold — This book is a collection of writings from early church notables and various people. The modern ideas of being part of the culture are strangely missing in this collection. This collection gives much in the way of support to the idea of separate kingdoms co-existing. These writers show us how they lived with the worldly kingdoms of their day but they did not intermingle nor allow the state to set the stage for them to minister.

With God On Our Side, By William Martin — This book is written by a man who is accepted by liberals but he gives a truthful, though very unflattering, view of the realities of the conservative political movement. We need not read only material from our own camp but we also must read the perspectives of those outside it to get a comprehensive view. This book is well written and full of authoritative documentation of where conservatism came from and what motivates it. I highly recommend it.

The False Presence Of The Kingdom, By Jacques Ellul — This writer is unknown to many church people in this country and certainly many conservatives. He gives us another perspective on the kingdom than either regular church teaching or the teachings of religious conservatives. This guy is a thinker but easy to read. His thoughts are well defined and stark. This author shows us that when we go along with the discussions of the world through their way of looking at the problems or under their terms we become one of them. We then fail to be a means of perspective for the world to see that there is something other than conservative or liberal. This alternative is the Kingdom of God.

Hope In A Time Of Abandonment, By Jacques Ellul — This book also is a mind opening experience. Ellul helps us to see that there are times of abandonment which God allows in order to get our attention. God's silence is evidenced by man's increasing verbosity. Man has never been more verbose than the modern religious conservative. With the continued failure of the conservative agenda we must conclude that this talk is not God speaking. Therefore this should be a clue to us to seek God out and come again to find our hope in Him during the time of abandonment.

Resident Aliens, By Stanley Hauerwas — Resident Aliens is a generally good book. The author encourages us to think about life and its engagements from a perspective outside of belonging to where or what we are involved with or living. We are living in the world but we are not supposed to be part of it in the means of going at life the way the world does. If they can see no difference between them and us there really is not any difference except in our minds. People cannot understand what they do not see in our lives. This book helps to give further perspective on this idea.

Sinner's In The Hands Of An Angry Church, By Dean Merrill — This book's title is a play on Jonathan Edwards' sermon: Sinners in the Hand of an Angry

God. This book was written by a former VP of Focus on the Family, one of the leading exponents of the Religious-Right conservative political ideology. Merrill confronts the historical inaccuracies that the religious movement is based on with solid facts and data. He confronts the faulty thinking of the religious conservative. The book does not go far enough to tell us in practical terms what we can do. Nor does Merrill deal with our true identity. The book is a succinct primer for gaining another point of view concerning Christians' involvement with politics in this country.

What the Cross Can Do That Politics Can't, By Erwin Lutzer — This book is not as rough and tumble as Dean Merrill's book. It does however buck the common ideas of the Religious-Right. It gives any open minded person the understanding that one can be Evangelical and not be a raving political maniac. Lutzer takes the reader in the direction of our true role and purpose as the Kingdom of God. This work is a bit less gritty than the *Diluted Church* but the author presents a good case for a different approach. I feel that Lutzer did not go far enough with his ideas nor did he do a background study of what motives lay under the approach of the religious conservative. I feel that this aspect is supremely important for a person to make the decision to go against the conservative right mindset but not give up on being biblical at the same time.

List of
Frequently Asked Questions

This section deals with questions that have come up in discussions while preparing this book. I have found that many times in discussion when it is discovered that I do not completely agree with the other person, that person often automatically assumes that I am 180 degrees opposite of them. The culture of our day commonly does this, seeking to try and convince the disagreeing person of the accepted position, even before there is a full understanding of the basis or degree of the seeming disagreement. This section will allow you to see that various questions can be dealt with straightforwardly in context to what has been written in the book.

As a format I will pose the question as they have been leveled at me. This book cannot address all these questions in its course because of the constraints of objectivity. The content of the book may raise some of these questions in your mind and I wanted to answer directly. I hope this sections clears the air and helps to deal with various details which may come up in the course of reading this book.

Question: Do you believe in total reclusion from secular culture, politics and society?

Answer: Scripture tells us that we are to be in the world according to John 17:15. So it is God's will that we maintain an interaction with the world. The question is then how much interaction is good and how much is too much. For this, only God can show us. If we are left to our own "interpretation" of a convenient few scriptures we will enter into fruitless, diluting activities that do not accomplish the purposes of God.

As far as culture, politics and society, these are mechanisms of human existence. These realms may be used for the purposes of the Kingdom. However, we should not focus on these as a, be all and end all. There are many other ways or means with which to influence people in society. Change does not happen through politics, society and culture. However, these will be changed if the people themselves are transformed.

Question: Do you think politics is an activity that is wrong or untouchable for a follower of Christ?

Answer: The Scripture again gives us examples of people who were involved with the politics of their day. It also gives examples of many more people who had nothing to do with politics. Some might say that because we have the opportunity in a "free society" that we should be good stewards. This puts more emphasis on our situation than it encourages us to depend on God for what He might want done. We cannot dismiss politics and declare it totally off limits, nor can we totally embrace it. We must seek God on what to do.

Further, we can see that Jesus did not bother Himself with the political affairs of the world in His day, neither did any of His disciples. The New Testament indicates a totally different idea concerning involvement in politics than the usual "pro" or "con" arguments heard so much today. Jesus indicated that His kingdom was *not of this world*. Therefore, if we put our new Kingdom in the forefront of our minds, identity, purposes and work we can enter into the mindset of co-existence with the world. We don't have to shut the world out nor do we need to plunge into its focuses and objectives.

Having said this we are free to pursue that which the Lord directs us to do in regards to political activity. If we concentrate on being the best at what God has gifted us to do, *a la* Joseph & Daniel, we will be brought before kings and princes and asked for our opinion and views. Our answers can be loaded with the truth God has given us. This in turn will influence the world for God.

Question: Is voting bad or evil?

Answer: I cannot see that scripture would declare or insinuate that voting is bad per se. Yet, this is only part of the analysis. To vote in a way that is uninformed would be bad. Many might think they are very well informed yet if they have not considered that politics is motivated by issues or how the issues are perceived, these same people potentially are duped into supporting things that are not really what they seem. This is a very real picture of politics and the conservative movement.

On a different front referendums and choices that are taken care of through a single vote pose a more direct means of effecting change. There is not the human failure element of carrying through on campaign promises as there is with voting for a person. If I vote for a person I may NOT get what I vote for. This is one particular weakness in voting people into office.

Question: Should one become educated about issues or is your point of view advocating obliviousness on these details for other focuses.

Answer: Scripture tells us to be wise as serpents and harmless as doves. It would seem that God is instructing us to be aware. Being aware however goes beyond knowing what people are saying about a subject. What motivates an issue and what are the consequences of supporting or not supporting an issue should be the details we consider.

Scripture tells us that God the Holy Spirit is ready to make us aware of what we need to do. Sometimes I think this detail is far under played in the conservative movement. Again, God will tell us what is good and necessary for us to do. We do not have to be motivated or manipulated by anything. If we respond to issues based upon anything else than God's direction we are being manipulated already. God is the only means of keeping us objectively involved and functioning in meaningful pursuits. Otherwise we become a pawn or a well-meaning but duped player in somebody else's game.

Question: What about standing up for righteousness? Don't we have an obligation to do this at least?

Answer: This all depends on how and by whose definition we are using. Who is framing the issue? Jesus said much about the Jews' attitude concerning the value of women and slavery without ever saying a word. When He took a towel and washed the disciples' feet, He demonstrated what He valued and believed by doing something consistent with His ideas. He did not demonstrate and negatively draw attention to what was wrong in society. He acted upon truth and showed truth in His actions. Christ did not respond to the issues as they were framed by society, just take a look at the story of the woman taken in the act of adultery.

Truth is dynamic and speaks out for us when we live it, not when we talk about it. If we live out of our kingdom and out of God's provisions, the world will either sit up and take notice, or it will crush us because of not wanting to face truth. Our job is not to make the world a moral place so that we can be comfortable while we are here, that would be selfishness. Our job is to hold up the morality God has given us by living it. Then the world can see what truth is and make a moral decision for themselves. Jesus *never* forced anybody to follow in His footsteps. Everyone was free to follow as they saw truth lived out before them.

Question: How about running for office. Is pursuing a political office good or bad in your opinion?

Answer: The Bible record gives us examples of people who occupied political positions in their day. Some would point to this and try to use it as a proof text to justify the heavy-duty pursuit of political power such as we see in the conservative movement today. Such examples in no way form a "proof text." This only shows us that political involvement is within God's means to use as an avenue. Politics is just one of many "means" that God can use.

You will note that there were only a few people within the time period of the Bible that were used by God in the politics of their day. Conservatives would be quick to say that the Bible characters did not have a representative form of government and so it was not possible to pursue political power. Hence, this is thought to be the reason for only a few people ever being involved with the governments of their day. This is a bit shortsighted. In saying this, such people are unwittingly devaluating the Bible's applicability to us in our day. Additionally, just because we have the opportunity politically, does not mean that this is what we should do. Since the Bible shows us that either involvement or non-involvement are biblically permissible means, God needs to guide us into what we can and should do.

Conservatives have other ideas in mind when they throw out a question like this one. Compulsory political involvement, if there is opportunity, is not mandated in scripture. This modern approach, which is selfishness covered up by a bevy of other motives, helps the activist see things the way they want to see them. The conservative will have a very difficult time using all of what scripture has to say on the subject of church/state relations, to base their reckless forays into the political arena to "dominate it for Christ."

Question: Isn't America special and perhaps God's tool in the world? Shouldn't we defend it from moral decay and try to continue its power for good?

Answer: America's founding was an amazing phenomenon, no doubt. This does not mean that America is any greater of an item in God's economy than any other nation. God blesses what He can bless. There is no Biblical indication that America is a special thing in God's view. God has a special place for only one nation, yet he loves all peoples. If we attribute any more significance to America because God has blessed it in the past we could be diverging from maintaining an identity in Christ's' kingdom to settling back into the world's mindset from which we were plucked.

The best way to stem moral decay, if this is really our concern, is to live differently, not to tell everyone else that they need to comply with our moral standards. To expect that others should comply with a moral standard based out of a relationship that they don't have is crazy! Morality can only be found in God. If you don't know Him all you can do is try to improve yourself by some arbitrary standard. To be concerned only with the moral decay and its effect on us is self-centered. The world is messed up because of sin and when people come to know truth in God, their living will be changed. Living in such a way as to lift up Christ to where people can see truth and are confronted with it is what we need to be concerned with. We cannot live this way if we are trying to take shelter in the world's establishment so as to assure our own comfort.

America may not always continue in the "blessedness" of its past. Especially when we consider "End-Times" we don't know for sure what role America will play nor whether we will be a part of the scene. If we do not maintain a freedom in mind set "to do" or "not to do" in reference to political interaction with the culture in America, we may already be directly cooperating with the enemy. If we are not listening to God we will be an unwitting pawn in the enemy's game in this world.

God has not outlined a "special" purpose for America in scripture nor does He have an eternal purpose for it. If we are following God, we won't put any more trust and purpose in

America's perpetuity than God does. If America fails to be used of God, are we more or less empowered or purposeful in our lives? I should say not! Yet, if we are focused on America's continuance we are being selfish as well as being diluted in our focus and purposes as followers of Christ.

Question: What about issues. How should we deal with them?

Answer: Many times there are real problems that need a response. Issues do have a real essence. It is these aspects we need to consider. However, we need to go to God for how to respond. If we respond to an issue as the world defines it or is using it we walk away from being God's tool. God has a way of meeting needs and taking care of problems in such a way that it draws people to Himself.

Issues by the way the secular world defines things are usually only a means to an end. Meeting these needs many times ends up only in meeting a temporary need without bringing people to confront their sin and lack of relationship with God. God's solution and the world solutions are rarely the same. Our focus needs to be on God and His will and timing, not man's. When we go about issues, just on the basis of their being presented to us, we may be running ahead of God. Notice that God does not answer all your prayers immediately

Question: Aren't you sticking your head in the sand and getting out of the world by not embracing the advantages of politics as cultural engagement?

Answer: Those that feel this way simply do not see that there are many other ways to engage the world.

Prayer seems to be a lesser means of engagement. Excelling at your ability or vocation
seems to be a lesser consideration. Dealing with
realities behind the issues, in a way that brings
honor to God and directs those affected to God,
does not seem to be widely considered. Going
about life from the perspective that we are
"Resident Aliens" and Ambassadors of God in
whatever part of the world we live does not
seem to be a comprehensive reality. Many studies show us there is no identifiable difference
between people who call themselves Christian
and the secularists around them that make up
the rest of society. There is something definitely
wrong with this picture. Somebody is not following what Scripture says or what Christ is
telling us.

Question: Isn't your idea of "disengagement" what
brought us to the mess that society is in
today?

Answer: Absolutely not! Many activists and theo-
retician make this accusation and it is patently
naive. If one would read almost any comprehensive church history, they would see that there
were many groups/movements who disengaged
society from one perspective to reengage it from
a competing kingdom mindset. These groups
"co-existed" alongside of the worldly society as
a means of showing an alternative. They met
needs and provided services where the world
had no conscience about what was right or
wrong. Some of these groups include: the Moravians, Waldensians, Ultraquists and Hussites.
This list is in no way exhaustive.

In all fairness there were also exceptions
within the general lean of each group or movement named. The point is to draw attention to

people whose mind sets were far a field from our modern ideas but they were not opposite of us either. They were an alternative in their day as well as ours.

If the question of "disengagement" is being posed from the perspective of total and permanent self-ostracism from society then there are some further details that we need to address. However, if we disengage from one perspective to re-engage from another, there is plenty of NT support for this ideal. There is also tremendous amounts of post-biblical evidence that gives us more understanding of biblical application as well as evidence of success.

Question: How can we affect society if we do not focus on the societal means of exerting influence through politics?

Answer: How did Jesus do it? Does the same Spirit that lived in Him live in us? Did Jesus' followers use political means in the way we think of using it to exert influence?

The scripture is replete with examples of people not using the politics of their day to do God's work. The scriptures also have accounts of God directly using His people in the politics of their day to do His will. The point is, that in either case of involvement or non-involvement, God was directing what was done. Those who say we have to use politics are as imbalanced as those who say we can't. The real question is what is God directing us to do at this point?

Bibliographies

Chapter 1 Subjective Thinking In The Camp

1. http://www.answersingenesis.org/home/area/faq/dating.asp (accessed May 2001)
2. Jacques Ellul, False Presence of the Kingdom, 1972 (Seabury Press) pg. 95

Chapter 2 The State Of The Church In America

1. George Verwer quoted by: Dean Sherman on 2nd side of tape 2   Series on Balance, YWAM 1-800-922-2143
2. Keith Green, Why YOU should Go To The MISSION FIELD. Available through: Last Days Ministries, 825 College Blvd. Suite 102 #333, Oceanside, CA 92057-6258 See: "Articles Index" page of the Web Site www.lastdaysministries.org
3. George Barna, The Second Coming of the Church, 1998 (Word Publishing, Nashville, London, Vancouver, Melbourne) pg. 3
4. Keith Green, Why YOU Should Go To The MISSION FIELD. Available through: American Tract Society, P.O. Box 462008, Garland, TX 75046-2008
5. US Center for World Missions web-site and corroborated with David B. Barrett & Todd Johnson with Global Evangelism Movement at http: www.gem-werc.org (accessed Oct. 2004)
6. Global Evangelism Movement at http: www.gem-werc.org (accessed Oct. 2004)
7. George Barna, The Second Coming of the Church, 1998 (Word Publishing, Nashville, London, Vancouver, Melbourne) pg. 6
8. World Christian Encyclopedia, 2nd Ed. pg, 5 & 8
9. Ibid.
10. Ibid.
11. Ibid.
12. George Barna, The Second Coming of the Church, 1998 (Word Publishing, Nashville, London, Vancouver, Melbourne) pg. 2
13. Ray Comfort, Hell's Best Kept Secret, (Whitaker House, 30 Hunt Valley Circle, New Kensington, PA 15068) pg. 9
14. Servant Magazine, Spring 2001 pg. 8 Quoted from Neil Pirolo book Serving as Senders.

15 Servant Magazine, Fall 2000. Compiled from U.S. Center for World Missions, in Charisma Magazine Phil Bogosian says it is only .025%.
16 Servant Magazine, Spring 2001 pg. 8 Quoted from Neil Pirolo book Serving as Senders.
17 George Barna's web-site: www.barna.org Go to past publishing on: Evangelism (accessed Aug. 2004)
18 Ibid.
19 Ibid.
20 George Barna's web-site: www.barna.org Go to past publishing on: Politics (accessed Aug. 2004)
21 Ibid.

Chapter 3 Stupid Is As Stupid Does

1. William Martin, With God on our Side, (Broadway Books, 1996) pg. 97.
2. Ibid. pg. 147
3. Phyllis Schlafly, A choice not an Echo, (Pere Marquette Press, P.O. Box 316, Alton, IL, 1964)
4. William Martin, With God on our Side, (Broadway Books, 1996) pg. 81
5. Cal Thomas, Blinded by Might, (Zondervan Publishing House, Grand Rapids, MI: Div. of Harper Collins, 1999) pg. 22
6. William Martin, With God on our Side, (Broadway Books, 1996) pgs. 310-311
7. Cal Thomas, Blinded by Might, (Zondervan Publishing House, Grand Rapids, MI: Div. of Harper Collins, 1999) pgs. 23-25

Chapter 4 How Did We Get Here Anyway

1. George Barna, The Second Coming of the Church, 1998 (Word Publishing, Nashville, London, Vancouver, Melbourne) pg. 25
2. Ibid. pg. 4

Chapter 5 Theology As A Motivator For Political Activism

1. Quoted from J. A. Comenius' work, *Unum Necessarium*, by: E.H. Broadbent in Pilgrim Church pg. 138-139
2. Bill Bright, in the foreword to Save America, by H. Edward Rowe, (Fleming H. Revell)

Chapter 6 History As A Motivator For Political Activism

1. Doug Bandow, Beyond Good Intentions, 1988 (Crossway Books, Wheaton, IL) pg. 28
2. Jan Amos Comenius, The Labyrinth of the World and the Paradise of the Heart, 1998 (Paulist Press, Mahwah, NJ 07430) pg. 110-111
3. Jacques Ellul, Hope In A Time of Abandonment, 1973 (Seabury Press) pg. 145

Chapter 7 Mis-Identity As A Motivator For Political Activism

1. Bob Sjogren, Unveiled at Last, 1992 (YWAM Publishers, Seattle WA 98155) pg. 56
2. Eberhard Arnold, The Early Christians, Baker Book House 1979 pgs. 77-82

Chapter 8 We Are "Caesar" Or Are We

1. A. Ralph Epperson, Unseen Hand, 1998 (Publis Press Tuscon, AZ) pg. 36
2. Richard Wurmbrand, Tortured for Christ, 1998 (Living Sacrifice Book Co. Bartlesville OK 74005-2273) pgs. 15-16

Chapter 9 The Deceptiveness Of Democracy

1. John Bunyan, Pilgrim Progress, (public domain)
2. Richard John Neuhaus, The Naked Public Square, 1986 II-ed. (Eerdmans Publishing Co. Grand Rapids MI 49503) pg. 30
3. Doug Bandow, Beyond Good Intentions, 1988 (Crossway Books, Wheaton IL) pg. 223

Chapter 10 Other Concerns About Politics

1. Cal Thomas, Blinded by Might, 1999 (Zondervan Publishing House, Grand Rapids, MI: Div. of Harper Collins) pgs. 210-211
2. Dean Sherman, Spiritual Warfare, 1990 (YWAM Publishers, Seattle WA 98155) pg. 152
3. Leonard Verduin, Reformers and Their Stepchildren, 1964 (Wm. B. Eerdmans Publishing Co. Grand Rapids MI 49503) pg. 212
4. Keith Green recorded, release on, For Him who has Ears to Hear   Album as a preface to "Draw Me".
5. Felix Bovet, Count Zinzendorf, 1893 Reprinted by Harvey Christian Publishers, UK pg. 66

Chapter 11 So What

1. Stanley Hauerwas, Resident Aliens, 1989 (Abingdon Press, Nashville TN 37203) pg. 115
2. Doug Bandow, Beyond Good Intentions, 1988 (Crossway Books, Wheaton IL) pg. 28
3. Felix Bovet, Count Zinzendorf, 1893 Reprinted by Harvey Christian Publishers, UK pg. 59
4. Quoted of Ezra Taft Benson, by Stephen Covey, The 7 Habits of Successful People, pg. 309
5. Quoted by Paris Reidhead, attributed to the Moravian Brethren, from a sound recording called Ten Shekels and a Shirt, available in written and digital forms on the internet.

Chapter 12 Where Do We Go From Here

1. William Gould, Christian Statesman Vol. No.142 #5 P.O. Box 8741-WP, Pittsburgh, Pennsylvania 15221
2. Richard Wurmbrand, (Diane Books, reprinted in 1976, Glendale, CA) pg. 72. (Notice this is quoted from an earlier edition of Wurmbrand's book. More recent editions have tamed this statement and exclude mentioning fundamentalism as fourth generation 'truth'.)
3. Stanley Hauerwas, Resident Aliens, 1989 (Abingdon Press, Nashville TN 37203) pg. 48

Chapter 13 Seeing Our Struggle Correctly

1. Leonard Verduin, Reformers and Their Stepchildren, 1964 (Wm. B. Eerdmans Publishing Co. Grand Rapids MI 49503) pg. 215

2. Ibid. pg. 135
3. Cal Thomas, Blinded by Might, 1999 (Zondervan Publishing House, Grand Rapids, MI: Div. of Harper Collins) pg. 94
4. Ibid. pg. 23
5. Dean Sherman, Spiritual Warfare, 1990 (YWAM Publishers, Seattle WA 98155) pg. 112
6. Leonard Verduin, Reformers and Their Stepchildren, 1964 (Wm. B. Eerdmans Publishing Co. Grand Rapids MI 49503) pg. 31
7. Keith Green, lyrics from the Album: Make My Life A Prayer To You, (Sparrow Records) track-4

Chapter 14 What Are We More Than Others
1. Richard Wurmbrand, Alone With God, 1999 Living Sacrifice Books Bartlesville OK. 74005-2273, pg. 35

Chapter 16 Comparing Ideas Of Citizenship
1. Lesslie Newbigin, The Other Side of 1984, 1983 (Church House Publishing, Cambridge, UK) ISBN 28254-0784-4, pgs. 13-15
2. Mathetes (or Disciple) in his epistle to one Diognetus. Thought to be written in A.D.130. From: THE ANTE-NICENE FATHERS The Writings of the Fathers down to AD 325. Compiled and edited by The Rev. Alexander Roderts, D.D., and James Donaldson, LL.D. (Ages Digital Master Christian Library Version.5) pgs. 58-60

Chapter 17 How Then Shall We Live
1. Leonard Verduin, 1964 (Wm. B. Eerdmans Publishing Co. Grand Rapids, MI 49503) pg. 24
2. Larry Crabb, The Marriage Builder, 1982 (Zondervan Publishing House, Grand Rapids, MI 49506) pgs. 52-57
3. Jacques Ellul, False Presence of the Kingdom Seabury Press 1972 (Seabury Press) pg. 95

Postscript:
1. Leonard Verduin, Reformers and Their Stepchildren, 1964 (Wm. B. Eerdmans Publishing Co. Grand Rapids MI 49503) pg. 276
2. Bob Sjogren, 1992 (YWAM Publishers, Seattle WA 98155) pg. 17.
3. Leonard Verduin, Reformers and Their Stepchildren, 1964 (Wm. B. Eerdmans Publishing Co. Grand Rapids MI 49503) pg. 278

Concepts Used by Author

Other Material By Author

I have recently started a pamphlet series entitled: *The Kingdom Citizenship Series*. This is an effort to give specific application to being an alternative to either the religious community's view of dominating the political arena or society's ideas of replacing the church from either a conservative or liberal mind set.

So little is available to the believer regarding our citizenship in Heaven and the rigors of being a light rather than a loud-mouth. We need to cultivate the concepts of respect for the secular world around us because they have as much right to their view as we do. We need to learn again how to influence people.

Volume 1, The Kingdom Of God Amongst The Kingdom Of Men: What Is Our True Identity

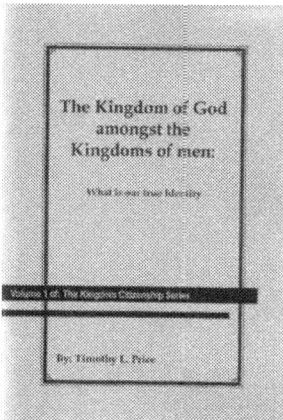

This work is a boiled down rendition of: *The Diluted Church*. Since our identity is vastly misunderstood in the modern church, our living, which will come out of this incorrect view, will be off-base.

We need to understand who we are so that we can begin to live like Christ. We need to die to who we were before Christ. This booklet is good to get the basics of *The Diluted Church* in a very succinct reading.

There are newer issues already available. Please visit: http://www.kingdomcitizenship.org/resources/ pamphlets.htm There these items and more materials available are to purchase and download at this site.

Another book in progress

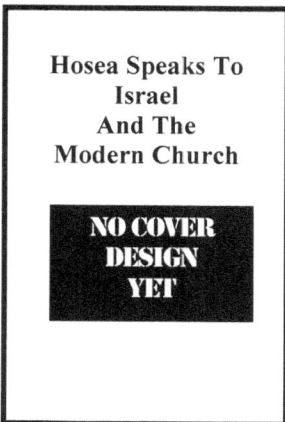

This work will be a commentary and teaching based from the Old Testament book of Hosea. Today the book of Hosea is rarely sought after for teaching, insight or direct application in modern situations. However, the book of Hosea has much to say to us today. This book will be due out in late-2006. On top of the commentary material this book will be study material, charts, appendix and material for any reader who wants to become more aware of what God has to say about our "modern" situation today.

www.ingramcontent.com/pod-product-compliance
Lightning Source LLC
Chambersburg PA
CBHW021047090426
42738CB00006B/217